LAND OF MY FATHERS

Evan James : Ieuan ab Iago
1809 – 1878

James James : Iago ab Ieuan
1833 – 1902

Land of my Fathers

Evan, James, their lives and times

Gwyn Griffiths

First impression: June 2006

Copyright: Gwyn Griffiths/Gwasg Carreg Gwalch 2006

ISBN 1-84524-061-8

Cover design: Alan Jôs, Stiwdio 23, Caernarfon
Printing: Gwasg Dwyfor, Penygroes

Photographs: Gwyn Griffiths, Pontypridd Town Museum
and the National Library of Wales

 Heritage
LOTTERY FUNDED
Supported by the Heritage Lottery Fund

Published by
rreg Gwalch, Llanrwst
)1492 642031

Hen Wlad Fy Nhadau

Mae hen wlad fy nhadau yn annwyl i mi,
Gwlad beirdd a chantorion enwogion o fri,
Ei gwrol ryfelwyr, gwladgarwyr tra mad,
Dros ryddid collasant eu gwaed.

Gwlad, Gwlad, pleidiol wyf i'm gwlad.
Tra môr yn fur i'r bur hoff bau,
O bydded i'r heniaith barhau.

Hen Gymru fynyddig, paradwys y bardd,
Pob dyffryn, pob clogwyn, i'm golwg sydd hardd,
Trwy deimlad gwladgarol mor swynol yw si
Ei nentydd, afonydd i mi.

Gwlad, Gwlad, pleidiol wyf i'm gwlad.
Tra môr yn fur i'r bur hoff bau,
O bydded i'r heniaith barhau.

Os treisiodd y gelyn fy ngwlad dan ei droed,
Mae heniaith y Cymry mor fyw ag erioed,
Ni luddiwyd yr awen gan erchyll law brad,
Na thelyn berseiniol fy nglwad.

Gwlad, Gwlad, pleidiol wyf i'm gwlad.
Tra môr yn fur i'r bur hoff bau,
O bydded i'r heniaith barhau.

TRANSLATION

The Land Of My Fathers

The land of my fathers, the land of my choice,
The land in which poets and minstrels rejoice;
The land whose stern warriors were true to the core,
While bleeding for freedom of yore.
> Wales! Wales! favourite land of Wales!
> While sea her wall, may nought befall
> To mar the old language of Wales.

Mountainous old Cambria, the Eden of bards,
Each hill and each valley excites my regards;
To the ears of her patriots how charming still seems
The music that flows in her streams.
> Wales! Wales! favourite land of Wales!
> While sea her wall, may nought befall
> To mar the old language of Wales.

My country though crushed by a hostile array,
The language of Cambria lives out to this day;
The muse has eluded the traitors' foul knives,
The harp of my country survives.
> Wales! Wales! favourite land of Wales!
> While sea her wall, may nought befall
> To mar the old language of Wales.

(The above rendition by Ebenezer Thomas (Eben Fardd) was the first of many attempts to translate Hen Wlad Fy Nhadau into English. We have no date for the translation but it is likely that it was in print as early as 1858. Like the many subsequent efforts it enjoyed no success.)

i
Alaw Mia, Leah Non,
Daniel Morgan, Steffan Llŷr
ac Elan Gwen

Preface

This book was commissioned by an old friend and onetime colleague, the late Dafydd Meirion, Llyfrau Llais. Publishing in Wales has lost a dynamic personality of great vision. It is with great personal sadness that I realise that he did not live to see the publication of this book in which he invested so much time and enthusiasm. My sympathies and thanks go to Alys who allowed the publication of the book to go ahead in difficult circumstances.

I owe a great debt to Alan Jones, Stiwdio 23, for his act of faith in continuing with the work, meticulously and cheerfully. It became a pleasure to work with him. Thanks, too, to Myrddin ap Dafydd, Gwasg Carreg Gwalch, who generously picked up the project and ensured that the book saw the light of day. I feel sure that the composers of our National Anthem would have appreciated, as much as I do, the contribution of Alan and Myrddin!

My thanks to descendents of the family of Evan James (Ieuan ab Iago) and James James (Iago ab Ieuan) for their kind assistance and interest – in particular Mrs Barbara Jenkins, Kenfig Hill, Dr David Williams, Bargoed, and Thomas Taliesin Leyshon whose book linking the histories of the James family and that of William Edwards, builder of Pontypridd's celebrated bridge, was invaluable.

I am hugely indebted to Brian Davies, Curator of Pontypridd Museum, for many valuable and interesting suggestions and practical assistance.

Likewise, I owe a great debt of gratitude to Dr Meredydd Evans and Ms Phyllis Kinney for their generosity in sharing their invaluable knowledge with me. Also to Daniel Huws, former Head of the Department of Manuscripts at the National Library in Aberystwyth.

Thanks to Nicholas Walker and Mrs Lowri Jenkins of the Museum of Welsh Life, St Fagan's, for their ready assistance and patience; likewise to the ever-helpful Hywel Matthews of Pontypridd Town Library; and the staff of the Department of Manuscripts at the National Library.

Thanks also to Tim Saunders for checking the Irish and Cornish translations of *Hen Wlad Fy Nhadau* and to Brian Stowell for his assistance with the Manx version.

My sincere thanks, also, to my wife, Gwen, who spent many hours with me struggling to decipher the lovely, but often tiny, handwriting of Evan James.

Gwyn Griffiths
Pontypridd

Contents

Introduction

Hen Wlad Fy Nhadau (*Land Of My Fathers*) stands proudly among the finest and most stirring anthems of the world. Yet it was composed by two modest tradesmen, a father and son, from a family of weavers and publicans who plied those crafts and trades in what was a small but expanding town in Wales's industrial southeast. In 1856, the year they composed their song, Pontypridd was a small town, mostly Welsh-speaking, with the wave of incomers that changed it into the most Anglicised of South Wales towns yet to come.

It is a romantic song of love and praise for a pre-industrial Wales – the old rural Glamorgan and Gwent, to be precise. The first line with its simple pronouncement of endearment to the ancient *Land of my Fathers*. We are told that it is a land of poets and singers; then we are reminded in a couple of lines of battles past and warriors who spilt their blood in the cause of freedom, as the music moves from the romantic to a more military rhythm. The second, seldom sung, verse praises Wales's mountains, its valleys, crags, streams and rivers. There is none of the strident nationalism we associate with some national anthems. We are in the third verse before we get a hint of nationalism, yet again Evan James tempers his message. The rape and violence of the enemy alone was not responsible for Wales's loss of freedom and independence, there was also the "terrible hand of treason". The Welsh themselves must accept a degree of responsibility. Evan had read his history books. Yet he remains optimistic. The muse is fresh and virile and the harp has not been silenced.

And like a silver thread, in the chorus, we have Evan's love of the language – "*O bydded i'r heniaith barhau*" (may the language endure).

For a nation that well into the 20th century possessed few institutions and in the 19th century was devoid of any institutions except an increasingly Anglicised Eisteddfod, the language was the one symbol of a Welsh identity. Were it not for a language, to differentiate Wales from England there would be no National Assembly Government, no University of Wales, no National Museum, no National Library and no Welsh TV channel. It was this loyalty to language that welded us together into one nation. Even though only about a fifth of the population can speak the language, the other 80 per cent must accept that without it Wales would be a much poorer nation – institutionally as well as culturally. Evan James appreciated the importance and the significance of Welsh in his own time; whether he anticipated its continuing importance in the following century is debatable. And if some of the leading lights of 19th century Wales kowtowing to Queen and Country (in their case, England) were uncomfortable with a song proclaiming a passionate desire for the old language to endure, it struck a chord with the working class – "y werin" – that transcended two centuries.

Anthems are composed when there is a need to stir up patriotic or nationalist fervour, often in times of war. They are songs to inspire men to war, to reflect national pride, celebrating victories in battle. The mid-19th century was a time of intense nationalistic fervour. Welsh patriotism was struggling to survive in the face of a massive surge of the British (English) nationalism of an Empire at the peak of its powers. In spite of the danger of being swamped by the nationalism of its aggressive next-door neighbour for Wales it was also a productive century, particularly in literature and music, even in artistic endeavours like art and sculpture not usually associated with the Welsh tradition. The Eisteddfod, locally and nationally, was gaining popularity, and moving from being the preserve of the poets to be more musical with the mass appeal of large choirs. The report of the 1847 Education Commission – often referred to as The Treason of the Blue Books – portraying the Welsh as barbaric, uneducated and immoral whipped the nation into a fury. The three commissioners were English, Anglicans, understood no Welsh and had no sympathy for noncomfomity. While there was in Wales a level of literacy far higher than in many parts of England, they were literate in Welsh, not the language of the commissioners. That literacy was due to the Sunday Schools and the continuing influence of Griffith Jones's Circulating Schools which in the mid to late 18th century had given Wales a high level of literacy, attracting interest from far and wide – Catherine the Great of Russia commissioned a report on them. Many of the private day schools by the 1840s, however, were of a poor standard with Welsh children taught in English by teachers who themselves did not possess a good understanding of that language. Many meetings were held in the Rhondda and Cynon Valleys, Pontypridd and Merthyr protesting about the report, and as will be shown later Evan James himself was angered by its one-sided unfairness. The *Blue Books* stirred a wave of angry nationalism that may well have contributed to a desire for a National Song for Wales.

John "Ceiriog" Hughes's words *I Wisgo Aur Goron* (To Wear a Golden Crown) sung to the tune *Glan Medd-dod Mwyn* (The Verge of Sweet Intoxication) had become quite popular – it was sung at the great Llangollen Eisteddfod of 1858, the same Eisteddfod that brought *Hen Wlad Fy Nhadau* to the attention of the nation. Others had the ambition to write "a national song". A year before *Hen Wlad Fy Nhadau* was composed John Jones (Talhaiarn) published in a book of verse a poem with the title *Gogoniant i Gymru* (Glory to Wales) to be sung to the tune *Llwyn Onn* (The Ashgrove). He made no direct reference to the language, but praised the muse and the harp, the beauty of Wales's mountains and valleys, "every river, and estuary, every grove and lake" and of brave princes fighting for freedom.

May be it was the melody composed by the harpist, weaver and later publican James James that immortalized Evan's words. Or that "the father and son from Pontypridd through a perfect fusion of the muse of one and the music of the other" as is said on their memorial stone in Ynysangharad Park, Pontypridd, who gave "of their gentle love for Wales the nation's anthem". As will be seen, there remains the mystery as to whether it was the poem or the music that came first. It should also be said that others played a part in popularising the song – Llewelyn Alaw of Aberdare who included it in his entry for a collection of unpublished songs for the Llangollen Eisteddfod of 1858; Owain Alaw of Chester the adjudicator of that competition who was mesmerized by the song and made a vital contribution by promoting it in North Wales; and the choirs, Eisteddfod audiences and rugby crowds who played a part in reducing and expanding the chorus out of its original 16 bars, and the climactic pause on *heniaith*, the anthem's last word but one.

Dr William Crotch (cited by Sir Alfred T. Davies in a lecture at the unveiling in 1941 of a tablet of thanks to the father and son from Pontypridd for their gift to the Welsh nation in the Ceiriog Memorial Institute, Glyn Ceiriog) wrote in his *Specimens of Various Styles of Music* that "... the military music of the Welsh seems superior to that of any other nation." Sir Alfred continued: "Be that as it may ... the air composed by this humble father and son has the merit of not being worried

Ysgol Gymraeg Evan James

by too much noise, nor vitiated by vulgarity, nor marred by over-strained patriotism. It has been said of it, also, that in it there is 'a sufficiency of rhythm without injury to the dignified character of the whole composition'."

Hen Wlad Fy Nhadau is an unassuming song of praise, expressing without ostentation a simple love of Wales. It has no crass exhortation to take up arms, no entreaties for godly assistance to vanquish enemies. Strange as it may seem for a nation with a reputation for piety, the anthem makes no reference to God. This may explain past attempts to supplant it with Elfed's hymn *Cofia'n Gwlad Benllywydd Tirion* (Remember Our Country, Gentle Sovereign) and Lewis Valentine's words *Dros Gymru'n Gwlad* (For Wales Our Country) to the tune *Finlandia*. There have been many attempts to ditch it in favour of *God Bless The Prince Of Wales*.

This suggestion was last made, probably, in Debrett's List of Peers, 1970, and drew a waspish response from the *Daily Post* columnist Ivor Wynne Jones (August 18) that there could be no good coming from adopting the "*...sycophantic* **God Bless The Prince Of Wales**" adding that we already had a National Anthem and a perfectly good one, thank you very much.

Yet, not everyone agreed because in 1969 – the year of the Investiture – the Inter-college Eisteddfod had a competition to compose a new Welsh national anthem. The organisers argued that *Hen Wlad Fy Nhadau* had become a meaningless cliché, its singers unaware of the significance of the words they were singing. There were two entries – and the prize was withheld! Every effort to have it replaced has failed. Wales – Welsh-speakers and English-speakers – has stuck with it, and every attempt to provide an acceptable English translation has been a miserable failure. In the words of a friend, one of our best known writers, "There are two things that unite Wales, rugby and *Hen Wlad Fy Nhadau*." Adding that there can't be much wrong with an anthem that makes no reference to either God or royalty!

When the first commercial recording of Welsh songs was made in London on March 11, 1899, and released by the Gramophone Company, *Hen Wlad Fy Nhadau* was among those songs. The singer was a Madge Breeze, of whom nothing is known, except that she was the first in a long line of celebrated singers to record our anthem. She sang it briskly, quicker than the dignified pace with which it is usually sung today.

In 1905, when the New Zealand rugby team came to play Wales in Cardiff, a Tom Williams from Rhondda wrote a letter that was published in one of the Welsh papers suggesting the crowd should sing *Hen Wlad Fy Nhadau* before the match to counteract the *Hakka*. This was duly done, and the blood of the New Zealanders ran cold and Wales ran out winners. Sadly, it has not had quite the same effect since. But other countries were worried by the anthem's inspirational qualities. The English refused to play it at Twickenham, as did the Scots at Murrayfield, for a very long time. In 1975 at Twickenham, after the band played the Queen and walked off, the Welsh captain Mervyn Davies gathered his team in a circle and sang the Welsh Anthem. The crowd joined in. It was a moment of pure inspiration and Wales – as we did in those days – went on to win. *Hen Wlad Fy Nhadau* was never again ignored at Twickenham.

France had acknowledged the anthem in 1971. It was first sung before a France v Wales match in Paris on March 2 that year. The previous night, the brilliant broadcaster and commentator, Alun Williams, received a call from the conductor of the band that would be playing at the match the following afternoon. He did not have a copy of the music, and Alun hummed the tune to him over the telephone. It was not a completely successful operation. The band played it at a much livelier pace than Welsh crowds have become used to and finished a good four bars ahead of the supporters. Maybe someone had told the conductor that *Vivace* had been written above an early version of the tune.

In 1977, the dinosaurs of the English FA finally gave their permission for *Hen Wlad Fy Nhadau* to be played before an England v Wales match at Wembley – **before** the players came out onto the field! If the people of Wales had cherished the anthem and taken it to their hearts a hundred years earlier, a willingness to accept it by the international sporting community took much longer. We recall another of the late Alun Williams's efforts to ensure it received fair play, at the Commonwealth Games in Jamaica in 1966. Lord Swansea had won the Gold Medal in one of the shooting events. The medal presentation completed, the band struck up *God Save The Queen*. Alun Williams left his commentary position and ran across the field and stopped the ceremony. The conductor accepted he had made a mistake and as a breathless Alun Williams went back to his microphone the band started up again – with *Land of Hope and Glory*! Alun Williams rushed back and halted the proceedings again. This time there was a bit of an argument before the conductor eventually found copies of *Hen Wlad Fy Nhadau*. Lord Swansea had stood patiently on the rostrum all this time. It should be noted that the patriotic Alun Williams had spent his late teens in Pontypridd.

The weaver/poet and the innkeeper/harpist from Pontypridd had struck the right note. Almost by accident, they composed jointly an anthem that is both unassuming and stirring, a unifying anthem for an often fragmented nation. Composed by two men from a town in the valleys, the song became popular in its home town before being given a boost by a man from Aberdare, and a further huge injection towards acceptance by two North Walians – Owain Alaw, a music adjudicator and singer from Chester, and Isaac Clarke, a poet and publisher from Ruthin. Perhaps, in part, its popularity stemmed from the fact that both North and South played a part in its rapid rise to popularity. A charming and dignified song, its phrases and notes rising and falling, flowing like the mountains and vales, the rivers of the country and the waves that surround three of its sides. An anthem without arrogance or insult to others. A practical anthem anyone can sing with comfort in the key of E flat, all within the scope of nine notes, from D to the top E flat.

The names of Evan and James James would have been forgotten but for one song. They deserve better. Evan was a likeable man, cultured and retiring and a better poet than some of his contemporaries who published volumes of poetry. He wrote hundreds of *englynion*, the four line stanzas unique to the traditional Welsh metres, and many scores of poems to be read or sung at the dinners of *The True Order of Ivorites* and the Eisteddfodau of Glamorgan and Gwent. Less than a handful of those compositions ever appeared in print in any volume or literary magazine.

James was a collector of folk songs and until Dr Meredydd Evans made an interesting and valuable connection a few years ago, no one was aware of this priceless contribution.

They belonged to a large family of poets and harpists.

When I first came to Pontypridd in 1959 fewer than forty children attended Ysgol Gymraeg Pontsionnorton, the town's only Welsh medium school. By now a third of Pontypridd's children, from four to sixteen years of age, are educated through the Welsh language. In Mill Street, where Evan and James had their woollen factory when they composed the anthem stands the latest of those primary schools, Ysgol Evan James. It could have been named after the most famous pupil to walk its corridors in the days when it was a secondary school – Sir Geraint Evans. But it was unanimously agreed it should be named after the poet who wrote the words of the anthem. The school's motto is the anthem's last line, *O bydded i'r heniaith barhau* – may the old language endure.

The anthem is born

There are two basic, differing, versions of how *Hen Wlad Fy Nhadau* came to be written. The least complicated, which was confirmed in a letter by Taliesin, son of James James, composer of the melody, and grandson of Evan, was that James went for a stroll along the Rhondda road on a Sunday afternoon in January 1856 and that the tune came to him as he walked, inspired by "the rippling of the river". Mrs Barbara Jenkins, a great grand daughter of Taliesin James believes the date to have been January 6. Taliesin, in an interview granted to Lewis Davies of the *Western Mail* when he was 77, said his father was convalescing after being seriously ill with rheumatic fever and described the time as a Sunday *morning*! However, he rushed back to his father's house and factory – Tŷ'r Factory as it was known – in Mill Street, announcing:

"Father, I have composed a melody, which – I think – would be suitable for a Welsh patriotic song. Will you write some words for it?"

"Let me hear it," replied the weaver. The son hummed the tune and Evan said: "Go and get your harp." James, who lived a few doors from his father's home, got his harp and played the tune on it. Evan James was charmed by the music and he picked up a slate and a piece of chalk he kept near his loom – he was a poet, and a poet never knows when the muse may descend in the form of an image or a line of *cynghanedd* and began to write.

According to a letter written by Taliesin James, dated December 4, 1910, (see Appendix 1), the first verse was completed within minutes and the second and third verses in the morning. Taliesin's letter was addressed to a John Crockett in Pontypridd. It is very likely that the recipient of the letter was the son of the John Crockett who taught James James to play the harp. There was a John Crockett who in 1861 lived at No 1, Taff Street, probably on the corner with Mill Street, who was described as a mine owner, jeweller, clock and cabinetmaker. His son, of the same name, was also a clock maker and one of his clocks can be seen on the front of the gallery, facing the pulpit, in Pontypridd Museum.

When Mrs Elizabeth James, Evan's wife and mother of James, returned from Carmel Baptist Chapel, James was singing his father's words to his own harp accompaniment. Mrs James was a formidable lady, a fact that became evident when her body, and that of her much smaller husband, were exhumed and re-buried by the memorial to the composers in Ynysangharad Park, Pontypridd, in 1973. I think we can assume that she was fairly tolerant. She was a devout chapel-goer, but she appears to have accepted her husband's – and son's – associating with Myfyr Morganwg's Druidic Gorsedd at the Rocking Stone on Pontypridd Common. The utterances and activities of Myfyr and his Gorsedd did not enjoy the approval of the Pontypridd chapels. Tolerant or not, Elizabeth James saw this as a desecration of the Sabbath. James protested; had not David, King of Israel, played the harp on the Sabbath? To this she had no answer and the singing continued into the night. Taliesin James's letter says the second and third verses were written on Monday morning. Yet, he was telling Lewis Davies of the *Western Mail* that the first and second verses were written on the Sunday and the third verse on Monday.

A similar tale, with a few colourful embellishments, appear in a short article by a Daniel Owen, J.P., of Ash Hall, Cowbridge, which appeared in the November 1889 edition of the Welsh periodical *Cymru Fu*. Mr Huw Walters writes in *Cynnwrf Canrif* that this Daniel Owen (1829-1896) had once been an employee of the James's factory, before emigrating to

Australia where he made money before coming back to Wales and becoming a man of influence and importance in Cardiff and the Vale in the last quarter of the century. In *A Rattleskull Genius* Mr Walters also describes him as the owner of the *Western Mail*. This is what Daniel Owen wrote:

"I well knew both the writer of the words, and the composer of the music of our grand National Song, 'The Land of my Fathers'. The former was the late Mr Evan James, of Mill Street, Pontypridd, and the latter his son, James James. The inception of the idea of the song happened 36 years ago in this wise: -

"One Sunday evening Mr James James strolled out of his father's house, up Mill Street and along the banks of the River Rhondda, humming and whistling to himself an air which he was composing during his perambulations. Upon returning to his home he said to his father, 'I have composed some music, and I shall be glad if you will write some verses to it.' Before he wrote down a note of the music he went over the tune to his father. 'My boy,' said the father, 'fetch me a pint of beer from the Colliers' Arms, and I shall do it.' That excellent poet Mr Evan James always made it a point, although an abstemious man, to take a glass of beer before commencing to write his verses. The words and the music were composed that very night. This song is sung in every national gathering in the Principality, in America, in Australia, and wherever Welsh people do congregate. To my mind it is equal to 'God Bless the Prince of Wales' (composed by another Welshman, Brinley Richards) and equal even to 'God Save the Queen'. Mr Evan James has 'gone over to the majority' long ago, but his son James is still in the 'land of the living', residing in Mountain Ash. Is it not our duty as a Welsh nation to recognise in some practical way the genius of the neglected composer of the national song, which has thrilled the hearts of hundreds of our fellow countrymen?"

There exists, however, a more interesting – and appropriately romantic – version of the tale of how the anthem came to be composed. In his pamphlet *Our National Anthem*, the late Harri Webb, poet and nationalist, mentions a tradition in one branch of the family that Evan James had received a letter from a brother who had emigrated to the United States of America, praising the new country and urging the Pontypridd weaver and his family to follow in his footsteps to the land of great opportunities. A more detailed version of the story appears in a letter, dated October 25, 1962, sent by the Rev Gwilym Thomas, Penmaenmawr, to Evan and Blodwen James, Bellingham, Washington. It is clear from the letter that the Evan James living in Washington was a direct descendant of Evan James, author of the words of *Hen Wlad Fy Nhadau*. In his letter, the Rev Gwilym Thomas, who was born in 1870 and died aged 95 in 1965, explains that he is a grandson of Mary, an older sister of Evan James. He describes her as being the only sister of Evan James. This is not strictly accurate since there was another daughter who died in infancy. His letter describes a visit he paid with his mother to Evan James's home in Pontypridd a few years before the death of the weaver/poet – Gwilym Thomas says that he himself would have been about the age of four at the time. Evan noticed that his niece was pregnant and wondered if she would name the unborn baby, if a boy, after him. In a short while a baby boy was born and Gwilym Thomas's brother was duly named Evan James Thomas. Then we come to the interesting part of the letter:

"You, no doubt, know that you are not the first of the James's to emigrate to the United States. Two of your grandfather's brothers went there more than 100 years ago, John and James (it does appear that three brothers had emigrated, another brother named Daniel had also emigrated). They fought in the Civil War, one in the Army of the Northern

States, the other in the Army of the Southern States.[1]

"One of the brothers made a valuable contribution towards the composing of Hen Wlad Fy Nhadau. Mother told me that he wrote to your grandfather, and probably to the rest of the family praising the United States. He wrote of the New Country in glowing terms, of a country of great rivers, valleys and mountains and of great opportunities. He did not succeed. Your grandfather's reply was *Mae hen wlad fy nhadau yn annwyl i mi &c"*.

I am indebted to Dr David Williams, a retired General Practitioner living in Bargoed, for a copy of the Rev Gwilym Thomas's letter. David Williams's brother, incidentally, was the late Professor Phil Williams, an internationally renowned astronomical physicist, and Plaid Cymru member of the National Assembly of Wales. They, too, are descendents of Mary James. Dr David Williams, suggests – as does Gwilym Thomas's letter – that Evan James was not the only member of the family to have received a letter urging them to emigrate to America. Gwilym Thomas's son, the missionary Dr Emrys

---

[1]This is an interesting, if not relevant, footnote to the story of *Hen Wlad Fy Nhadau*. As well as the fact that three of Evan James's brothers had emigrated to America, the family believe that the Postmaster General Thomas Lemuel James who was on the platform of the Washington station when President Garfield was assassinated in 1881 was also connected to the family. Thomas L. James was born in 1831, and it is believed that his grandparents emigrated to America in 1800. If so, he could not have been a descendent of one of Evan James's brothers. Dr David Williams showed me a copy, handed down within the family, of Eva Hope's *Lincoln and Garfield*. The book contains a number of references to Thomas L. James, each one underlined in pencil – convincing proof that the family in the past were aware of a connection between him and the author and composer of *Hen Wlad Fy Nhadau*. Among the Evan James Manuscripts in the National Library of Wales I saw the address of a James James, Postmaster of Hazelton, Lucern, Philadelphia, although he would probably have been Evan's brother.

Thomas, said the exhortation came in the form of a poem and there is a suggestion that there was a kind of competition within the family to write a suitable response in verse.

Some of the brothers of the Evan James who wrote *Hen Wlad Fy Nhadau emigrated to USA along with others from that part. Somebody, of those who settled in USA, wrote a poem singing the praises of their new homeland, sent it back to Bargoed (probably to the pub). It stung the ones who had remained in Wales to write poems in praise of their homeland, and thus it came about that Evan James wrote* **Mae hen wlad fy nhadau yn annwyl i mi.**

As will be discovered later, this was a family of poets, singers and harpists.

We can imagine, as did Harri Webb, Evan James pondering over this invitation for many days, then on that Sunday, early in January 1856, taking his walk along the Rhondda road. Either he was feeling a necessity to make a choice between the old country and the new, or he may simply have felt the urge to respond to a poem received from the brother in America. Emrys Thomas suggests it was a poem in praise of the new country's vast expanse, its wide rivers, the beauty of its valleys and splendours of its mountains. The existence of this poem is no fanciful speculation or romanticising. Among the Evan James collection of manuscripts in the National Library in Aberystwyth there is the remnant of a letter, in Welsh, dated September 10, 1843, from James, one of the brothers in America. The letter is in the form of an imaginary dialogue, a short play, between Edward James – another of Evan's older brothers – and Mary at the gate of their home in Pontaberbargoed. In the dialogue the two are complaining that they have not, for a long time, received any news from the family in America. They are imagined as pondering what has happened to their relatives and should they write to them again as there has been no reply to their last letter. It can be read as a gentle admonishment to the family for neglecting to write. Although fragmented it is evidently a conscious attempt at producing a piece of literature.

Evan returns to his workshop and takes up the slate by the loom and sets out his reply, not as a letter, but as a poem. *Mae hen wlad fy nhadau yn annwyl i mi* ... (The land of my fathers is dear to me). He proceeds to describe the country, a land of poets and singers, of brave warriors who spilt their blood in the cause of freedom. Then, comes the refrain and the unambiguous response. *Pleidiol wyf i'm gwlad* – I pledge myself to my country. The word *pleidiol* has many connotations. The word *plaid* implies *party* in the political sense, *pleidlais* means *to vote*. He is throwing in his lot with the old country, giving it his allegiance. This may be the romantic version of how the words of the anthem were born – but it also seems the more likely of the two. A song direct in its message, expressed simply. They are words to be sung, simple lyrics, not an attempt at grand poetry. Evan was a skilled – if somewhat inconsistent – poet in the traditional Welsh metres. He was also fond of writing words to be sung to Welsh melodies and popular tunes of the day. In fact, he was a prolific poet, although I have yet to find more than a tiny handful of his poems published in the literary magazines of his day. He appears to have written purely for his own pleasure, without – regrettably – taking the trouble to polish his compositions. The lines of love for and in defence of his country flow easily. According to this version of the story Evan shows the words to his son and goes for an afternoon nap in bed. James now goes for a stroll along the river and after a while returns and calls in an excited voice to his father. "'Nhad, dewch lawr yn union!" ("Father, come down quickly!") Evan comes downstairs, half-dressed. James's face is lit up with

The Ancient Druid Inn on the outskirts of the village of Hollybush, near Argoed. It was here that Evan James had his woollen mill and inn before moving to Pontypridd

excitement. He sings the tune he has composed in his head as he walked along the river. Evan tells James to get his harp and after he has tuned it they both sing the new song together, refining the words and music as they go. When Mrs Elizabeth James returns from Carmel Chapel she reprimands them firmly for their lack of respect for the Lord's Day, but she is silenced by her son's response that David, King of Israel, played his harp on the Sabbath. The singing and the sound of the harp continued far into the night.

There is another little snippet to the story that on the Monday morning, Evan and James went next door, to No 13, Mill Street, the home of a Mrs Davies, and said to her, "We have written this song and tried it to the harp. Will you play it on the piano and sing it through?" Mrs Davies did so and said, "Marvellous, something will come of it!"

It will probably never be proved which story is the correct one. But with successful songs it is usual for the words to be written first with the melody following. Words give nuance and direction to the song. Did Taliesin James wish to highlight his father's contribution to the composition of the anthem? Was he reacting to the bitterness that followed the scurrilous accusations that the melody James had written was not original, but a plagiarised version of an old Scottish folk song? This part of the story of the anthem will be discussed later. However, Taliesin, in his letter, insisted that it was the music that came first.

The story is further complicated by a reference to the song in the second volume of *Hanes y Brytaniaid a'r Cymry* (The History of the Britons and the Welsh) by Gweirydd ap Rhys (Robert John Pryse) – published in 1874. Ap Rhys praises the contribution made by the poets in keeping alive the national spirit that "centuries of foreign government had failed to extinguish or weaken". He goes on: "The chord struck by the ancient poets and chroniclers played on in the hearts of their successors; and despite the closest proximity with their conquerors, they still speak the language of their country, cherishing its traditions, lovingly attached to its earth and land, and ready at all times to speak sincerely in the beautiful words of James of Pont y Pridd:–

> *Mae hen wlad fy nhadau yn annwyl i mi;*
> *Gwlad beirdd a cherddorion, enwogion o fri:*
> *Ei gwrol ryfelwyr, gwladgarwyr tra mad,*
>   *Dros ryddid gollasant eu gwaed:*
>   *Gwlad, gwlad! Pleidiol wyf i'm gwlad;*
>   *Tra môr yn fur i'r bur hoff bau,*
>   *O bydded i'r heniaith barhau!*

Os nad yw hen Gymru, fu unwaith mewn bri,
 Yn awr yn mwynhau ei holl freintiau;
Arafwch ychydig! dywedwch i mi,
 Pa wlad sydd dan haul heb ei beiau?
 Fy ngwlad, O fy ngwlad!
 Rhof iti fawrhâd,
 Dy enw sydd dra chyssegredig:
 O! rhowch i mi fwth,
 A thelyn neu grwth,
Yn rhywle yng Nghymru fynyddig.

Apart from the word *cerddorion* (musicians) for *cantorion* (singers) in the second line the first verse is as it is sung to this day. But this second verse, although expressing similar sentiments to the first, and for that matter with the other two verses of the anthem, as we know them today, differs in rhythm and structure. Did James, having been given the words, find it easier to compose music for the first verse, and Evan had then written two more verses to the same structure as the first?

Evidently there has been, in the past, some discussion about this second verse. Oswald Edwards in his A Gem of Welsh Melody refers to it as "the lost verse" and "the missing ten lines". Likewise, Harri Webb refers to "the 'lost' ten lines" and sees them as being "more explicitly political than anything that was retained but they contain also a hint of culturalist escapism and acquiescence." Webb suggests that the second verse confirms the case for the words having been written first in response to an invitation to emigrate to the USA. He goes further, suggesting that the words came first, inspiring a tune that in turn inspired more verses. While researching this book I found the "missing ten lines" included in another poem with the title *O Rhowch i Mi Fwth* (O Give Me a Cottage) which I have included, with a translation in the chapter of Evan's poems.

The events that follow are clearer. The father and son named their song *Glan Rhondda*, appropriately as it was composed on the banks of that river. A friend who has lived all his life in Pontypridd has pointed out to me that there was at that time a public house on the banks of the Rhondda called Glan Rhondda – and the song could have been named after a pub! We may recall that that best known of hymn tunes, *Cwm Rhondda*, was composed half a century later on the banks of the same river, a mile upstream, by John Hughes a clerk in the *Great Western Colliery*. The winding wheel to that colliery entrance, the *Hetty* as it is known locally, is still standing together with the 130-year-old engine still in working order and turned over from time to time by members of the Pontypridd History Society, who are renovating the site. Sadly, there are no such remains or ruins of Tŷ'r Factory, home of the father and son who gave Wales its anthem. We might remember, too, that in 1863 W. T. Rees (Alaw Ddu) – a friend of the Jameses - composed a hymn tune with the name of *Glan Rhondda*. By then the *Glan Rhondda* of Evan and James James had taken wings and gaining huge popularity in North and South Wales under a new name – *Hen Wlad Fy Nhadau*.

A popular song

It is believed that *Glan Rhondda* – or *Hen Wlad Fy Nhadau* – was first sung in public, within a month of being composed, in the Vestry of Tabor Methodist Chapel, now a Workingmen's Club, in Maesteg. The singer was 16-year-old Elizabeth John from Pontypridd, who was to marry John Davies (ap Myfyr), son of the colourful clock maker and Archdruid Myfyr Morganwg (Evan Davies). The same ap Myfyr who, many years later, wrote the splendid *Hir a Thoddaid* that can be seen on Evan James's gravestone. According to Mrs E. E. Parfitt, daughter of Elizabeth John, in a letter she wrote from Ohio in 1943, her mother's performance was heard by a professional singer, to whom she refers as Miss Miles, sister-in-law of the harpist John Thomas (Pencerdd Gwalia) of Bridgend. The same John Thomas who became harp tutor at the Royal Academy of Music and harpist to Queen Victoria – and harp tutor to Taliesin James, son of James James.

Mrs Parfitt wrote that Miss Miles had asked her mother for a copy of the song. Elizabeth John returned to Pontypridd and asked Evan James for a copy of the words and the music. He agreed, on the understanding that Miss Miles would sing the song in her next concert. There is no evidence that she did. James James, incidentally, had by then married Cecilia, daughter of Morgan and Joan Miles, tenants of Gellifonaches farm, Pontypridd. But there does not seem to be any connection between Miss Miles, the singer, and James's in-laws.

In an article in the *Western Mail* (April 4, 1884) the journalist and druid Owen Morgan (Morien) claimed that ap Myfyr was the first person outside the family to learn *Hen Wlad Fy Nhadau* and it was he who taught the song to Elizabeth John days after it had been composed. He also said

A drawing of Tabor Chapel, Maesteg. It was in the vestry, to the right of the chapel, that 16-year-old Elizabeth John of Pontypridd sang Hen Wlad Fy Nhadau in public for the first time

that it had been sung shortly after it had been composed by James James himself in an Eisteddfod held at the Castell Ifor Inn, Hopkinstown.

"It appears that the new hymn of Wales became immediately an object of much interest to the local vocalists," wrote Morien. "These, like the young composer himself, were comparatively self-taught in the divine art. They had been fascinated by those marvellous voices of past ages which the melodies of Wales had preserved on the tongues of a gifted peasantry among the rugged hills of their native land. These visited 'James's factory' nightly to learn the 'new tune'. It seems that the first man outside the young composer's family to learn the words and tune was 'ap Myfyr', the eldest son of the Archdruid. On those occasions young James invariably accompanied the voices with the harp. Soon afterwards an Eisteddfod was held at Ivor's Castle, Hopkinstown, a suburb of Pontypridd, and it was decided to introduce the song to the assembled bards and minstrels at that Eisteddfod. This was done by the composer himself with harp and voice ... On the morrow, after the Eisteddfod at Castell Ivor, the children of Pontypridd were singing the new melody about the streets, and from that day to this it has been spreading from land to land, and it is heard wherever Welshmen congregate."

Taliesin James in his letter to John Crockett makes similar assertions. "The song became exceedingly popular, so popular in fact, that even the children were soon singing and whistling it in the streets of Pontypridd." On June 21,1857, it was sung at Eisteddfod y Maen Chwŷf (The Rocking Stone Eisteddfod) by James James, accompanying himself – on the Rocking Stone itself according to Thomas Taliesin Leyshon, another descendant of the James family. (Evan James was a literary adjudicator at the same Eisteddfod). Copies of the words – but not the music – were produced by Francis Evans, Printer, Pontypridd, and sold in the manner of the old ballads in a four-page leaflet together with an English translation by

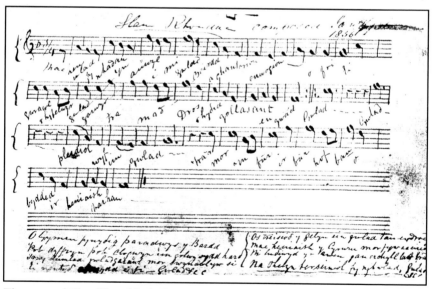

The score of Glan Rhondda in James James's own hand. ... But is this the oldest surviving copy?

Eben Fardd (Ebenezer Thomas). No date has been printed on the leaflet, although someone has written 1858 in the margin of the copy in Pontypridd Library. Eben, although from North Wales, had strong connections to, and a warm regard for, Pontypridd's colourful and eccentric literati, which suggests that the date 1858 could be correct. Neither his translation nor any of the numerous subsequent attempts at an English translation ever caught on and it may be revealing that the only successful and popular translations have been into Breton and Cornish, sister languages of Welsh.

The Great Llangollen Eisteddfod of 1858 was one of the most remarkable and colourful in the history of that institution. For the present, however, I will confine myself to what may have seemed an insignificant competition in a vast pageant of activities. A prize was offered for the biggest collection of unpublished Welsh melodies. A friend of James James, Thomas David Llewelyn (Llewelyn Alaw) from Aberdare, decided to try his luck at this competition. He called on James at his home in Pontypridd and asked him whether he knew any unpublished Welsh songs. According to Taliesin James he answered that he did not, but that a song he had composed – with the name *Glan Rhondda* – was becoming very popular locally. If Mr Llewelyn liked it he was welcome to include it in his collection, wrote Taliesin in his letter. Adding: "My father was weaving at the time, and he sang it to Mr Llewelyn from the loom, he (Mr Llewelyn) meanwhile sitting on a three-legged stool jotting down the notes". Llewelyn Alaw liked the song and included it in his collection, the collection which went on to win first prize at the Eisteddfod.

Llewelyn Alaw (1828 – 1879) was born in Llwydcoed, Aberdare. He was taught to play the harp at a young age and it is said that he was a proficient harpist by the time he was eight years old. At the age of eleven, he went with his father, to work underground in one of the Aberdare coalmines. He continued his musical interests and left the colliery in 1851 to pursue a comfortable life as a musician and poet. He was also an innkeeper for a time, the landlord of the appropriately named Harp in Mountain Ash. He became harpist to the Bruce family at Dyffryn. Henry Austin Bruce – later Lord Aberdare – had enough interest and knowledge of the Welsh language and its literature to translate into English, among other works, *Ymson y Bardd â'r Gog* (The Soliloquy of the Poet to the Cuckoo) by the poet and antiquarian from Llanystumdwy, Owen Gruffydd (1643 – 1730). Llewelyn also became harpist to the Aberpergwm family, in the Neath valley, home of Maria Jane Williams (1795 – 1873) whose pioneering collection, *Ancient National Airs of Gwent and Morgannwg,* won the Lady Llanofer prize at the Abergavenny Eisteddfod of 1837 and was published in 1840. It may be said that Llewelyn Alaw was continuing a rich tradition in distinguished company and if, as a collector, he did not measure up to the standards of Maria Jane Williams, his collection was valuable and the part he played in giving Wales a National Anthem may have been of greater significance than has been recognised. The Eisteddfod as an institution initiated some important collections of Welsh folk music. It also played its part – if not consciously – in the discovery and popularising of *Hen Wlad Fy Nhadau.*

Taliesin James's letter is quite clear that his father had told Llewelyn Alaw that *Glan Rhondda* was his own original work – not that this was of importance as the competition asked for a collection of unpublished songs. There was nothing to insist that those songs had to be **traditional**.

As can be seen from the scores of *Glan Rhondda* in Llewelyn Alaw's prize-winning entry and James James's personal song book in the National Library of Wales in

Aberystwyth, we have only the single line of the melody. Neither attempted to harmonise the tune. We can assume, as Dr Percy A. Scholes maintained, that James never wrote out any harmonisation, simply accompanying his singing, or that of others, by ear on his harp in the weeks and months after the song was composed. There is very little difference between the notes of James's version as set down in his personal song book (Llyfr Tonau Iago ab Ieuan, Evan James MSS, National Library of Wales) and Llewelyn Alaw's version (NLW 331) and how the anthem is sung today. Dr Meredydd Evans and Ms Phyllis Kinney, incidentally, are convinced that there are two versions of the tune in the Llewelyn Alaw collection, *Glan Rhondda* (NLW 331) and *Glan y Rhondda* (NLW 129B). It appears that Llewelyn Alaw's collection was to some extent dispersed over time. There are no words, for example, in the collection although Llewelyn Alaw's daughter, many years later insisted that his collection did include words. Anyhow, if there were no words, how was Owain Alaw able (see below) to publish them in 1860? Harri Webb (*Our National Anthem*) suggested that Llewelyn Alaw had arranged the tune for harp or piano. The tune as can be seen in the Llewelyn Alaw collection (NLW 331 and, indeed, 129B) prove that it was not so. If Llewelyn Alaw had hurriedly written down the song as James – working away at his loom - sang it to him, as Taliesin wrote in his letter, could Llewelyn on re-reading his notes have had some difficulties? Did he include, because of some uncertainty, two quite different versions in his collection? If this is so, Llywelyn Alaw's contribution to the evolvement of *Hen Wlad Fy Nhadau* may have been greater than we have realised!

The adjudicator of this particular competition at the Llangollen Eisteddfod was John Owen (Owain Alaw, 1821 – 1883) one of Wales's foremost musicians of his day. He was organist and choir master at St Mary's Welsh Church, Chester, a composer, and greatly in demand in Wales and beyond as an accompanist, Eisteddfod adjudicator and soloist. By all accounts he was a splendid baritone.

When he awarded the prize – £10 and a medal – to Llewelyn Alaw it was obvious that Owain had found one song in the collection quite charming, *Glan Rhondda*. As I have already noted, it appears that there were two versions of James James's tune in Llewelyn Alaw's collection, but we can forget the NLW 129B version for the time being. The main difference between the James version in his songbook, that of Llewelyn Alaw's collection and the way we sing it today is in the chorus. The number of bars in

> *Gwlad, gwlad,*
> *Pleidiol wyf i'm gwlad*

has been reduced from eight to five. Two "rest" bars, one after each *"gwlad"*, are no longer there. These rest bars, with no notes, would have given the harpist James James the opportunity to indulge in a *glissando* or *arpeggio*. Then the *"… gwlad; Tra"* is condensed into a single bar. This change from the more musically correct original eight bars to five bars must have been done by Owain Alaw when he published it under the title *Hen Wlad Fy Nhadau* in a book of songs with the title *Gems of Welsh Melodies*. Owain was also the first to arrange the song with piano accompaniment and to harmonise it for four voices, and for taking it down from James's original composition in the key of F to E Flat, making it more accessible to an Eisteddfod audience or – later – a crowd at a sporting venue. Harri Webb even made the suggestion that these little changes by Owain Alaw make the tune *"less the setting of a subjective lyric than a more objective, more public declaration."* The reason may well have been more prosaic. Owain was a soloist and before he published the song in his *Gems* he had been trying it out at concerts in North Wales and had quickly realised he had a popular song on his hands. It is probable that he realised that the song – from the point of view of the singer – moved on rather better without the rest bars after each "*gwlad*". Being a baritone, it could well have been his idea to take it down to E Flat, too. James James, a tenor, would not have concerned himself with such a matter.

Few, today, will be aware that Llewelyn Alaw was not the only person to submit an entry for the collection of unpublished Welsh melodies at the 1858 Llangollen Eisteddfod. There were two others – Caradog with eight tunes and Orpheus with 80. Enillwr Os Cyll, the pseudonym of the winning Llewelyn Alaw, had 125 tunes. Owain Alaw, while awarding the prize to Llewelyn Alaw, praised Orpheus's entry and recommended that he should be awarded £5 and that his entry, along with that of Llewelyn Alaw should be safeguarded. Yet in spite of this fulsome recommendation the identity of Orpheus remained a mystery. *Glan Rhondda* appeared in Orpheus's collection, too, with the note "*Written by a harpist named James James, Pontypridd*". This might suggest that the song was gaining popularity, or at least that the entry came from somewhere near Pontypridd. Or that James James himself was Orpheus! This revelation comes from Dr Meredydd Evans and his wife Phyllis Kinney, two internationally renowned folk music authorities. Other factors were taken into consideration but their theory is based largely on careful, scientific comparison of James James's writing and notation from his songbook with those of Orpheus. Dr Evans revealed his theory in an article with the title *Who was 'Orpheus' of the 1858 Llangollen Eisteddfod?* Published in the journal *History of Welsh Music*, Volume 5 (2002). In view of Owain Alaw's praise how was the identity of Orpheus concealed for so long? Did his friend from Pontypridd, Evan Davies (Myfyr Morganwg), collect the prize on his behalf? Myfyr, along with Dr William Price, played a prominent role in the Eisteddfod's colourful and eccentric opening ceremony. The significance of Dr Evans and Ms Kinney's revelations are considerable and will be discussed in full in the following chapter.

Owain Alaw must have assumed that *Glan Rhondda* was a traditional song. In 1860 he began publishing a series in four volumes of Welsh airs with the title

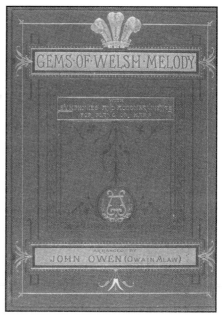

The first complete edition of the songs from the Gems

Gems of Welsh Melodies. It was a joint venture with the publisher and printer Isaac Clarke, Ruthin. Among the songs in the collection appeared *Hen Wlad Fy Nhadau* – the *Glan Rhondda* of Llewelyn Alaw's collection, now harmonised with accompaniment. According to Taliesin James it appeared in the third volume of the series. According to Lili Richards, former Head of Music at Ysgol Gyfun Gymraeg Rhydfelen, Pontypridd (manuscript in Pontypridd Library), it was in the second volume and it had on the page the words *Composed in January 1856 by Mr James James, Colliers Arms, Mountain Ash; Words by Mr Evan James, Pontypridd. English words with Symphonies, Accompaniment and Chorus by Owain Alaw.* It is obvious that Mrs Richards was not referring to the original edition, otherwise there would have been no cause for Evan and James to complain that they were given no credit for the song (see Taliesin James's letter, below and Appendix 1). Others – including Oswald Edwards (*A Gem of a Melody*) insist it was in the first series, and that would appear to be correct. According to Mr Edwards the first series was published in August 1860, the second in 1861, the third in 1862 and the last in 1864. There is certainly agreement on one point; it was the volume that included the song by the father and son from Pontypridd that sold best of all, by far. Although, as Oswald Edwards pointed out, the first series did include such popular songs as *Men of Harlech, The Break of Day* and *The Ashgrove*. The positioning of *Hen Wlad Fy Nhadau* in the seventh place in the order of songs suggests that Owain Alaw, although he had market-tested it in numerous concerts between 1858 and 1860 was not totally confident that he had in his hands such an inspirational song. That, or he did not have the confidence to back his hunch and place it in a more prominent position in his book.

The printer and joint-publisher of *Gems of Welsh Melodies* was Isaac Clarke, 6 Well Street, Ruthin. Oswald Edwards (*A Gem of a Melody*) has an interesting and valuable chapter on this forgotten man of Welsh printing and publishing. As well as being a printer of considerable skill and vision – he printed *Ceinion Alun*, the verses of the poet and clergyman John Blackwell, sermons, history books, and volumes of popular songs – he also wrote the Welsh hymn

> *Cyduned nef a llawr*
> *I foli'n Harglwydd mawr*
> *Mewn hyfryd hoen.*

> (Let heaven and earth unite
> In praise of our great Lord
> In vivacious joy.)

It can still to be found in modern Welsh hymnals, usually with the line that it is an adaptation of an English hymn by James Allen.

He deserves a place in the history of *Hen Wlad Fy Nhadau* as he was the first to print the anthem, the words and the music. The first three series of *Gems of Welsh Melody* were published in one volume in 1862 and a further edition – published jointly by Hughes and Son, Wrexham, and Simpkins & Marshall, London, appeared some years later although it was still possible to buy the "series" separately. Clarke lost money on the first venture, was declared bankrupt and died a poor man aged 51 in 1875. According to Oswald Edwards the first series had been priced too cheaply.

The *Gems*, interestingly, contained two English translations of *Hen Wlad Fy Nhadau*, one by Owain Alaw and the other by Eben Fardd – the one that appeared on the leaflet published by Francis Evans, Pontypridd. This proves that Eben Fardd's translation at least pre-dated 1860 and that the 1858 date scribbled on the copy of the leaflet in Pontypridd Library could be correct. Eben won the Chair at the 1858 Llangollen Eisteddfod for an ode on the title *Brwydr Maes Bosworth* (Battle of Bosworth Field). Did he have his attention drawn by someone to the song of the father and son from Pontypridd? Eben was on good terms with the poets of Pontypridd and had made a special request to be invested a member of Myfyr Morganwg's Rocking Stone Gorsedd *in absentia* in 1854. And publicly castigated for his folly by John Jones (Talhaiarn) at the Morriston Eisteddfod very soon afterwards. Although Ieuan Glan Geirionydd at the Liverpool Eisteddfod of 1840 had invested him into the bardic orders, Eben did not consider that any Gorsedd but that of Glamorgan and Gwent had the authority to bestow such an honour. It is also known that he adjudicated at an Eisteddfod in Merthyr Tydfil in 1850.

It is understandable that the name *Glan Rhondda* would have meant nothing to Owain Alaw; he would not have known anything of its history, where and how it was composed. When he first published it he must have assumed it to be a traditional song rescued from oblivion by Llewelyn Alaw.

The grave of the conductor Caradog (Griffith Rhys Jones) in Aberdare. Caradog was the first to conduct a performance of Hen Wlad Fy Nhadau sung by a choir in four-part harmony and accompanied by a string orchestra. Caradog, as leader of the orchestra, conducted the performance in Hen Dŷ Cwrdd, Aberdare, on New Year's Day 1860

"My father and grandfather protested about this and Owain Alaw apologised to them and explained how the song came to be inserted in the Gems," wrote Taliesin James in his letter to John Crockett. Owain sought and obtained permission from Evan and James to continue publishing the song, which he had renamed *Hen Wlad Fy Nhadau*. Some years later, according to Taliesin, Owain Alaw offered to buy the copyright and offered James James £15 worth of copies of his song *"Mae Robin yn swil"* as payment.

"Don't you think this was gross impertinence, after selling hundreds of copies … of the Gems of Welsh Melodies?" wrote Taliesin. "Mr Hughes of Wrexham, who published the

Gems of Welsh Melodies for Owain Alaw called at the Factory, Pontypridd, on one occasion and told my father that more copies of vol. 3 had been sold than vols 1 and 2 put together. Mr Hughes presented my father with the 3 vols and this is all he ever got for his song. Nothing from Owain Alaw who must have made hundreds of pounds out of my father and grandfather's song."

Ironically, the Llangollen Eisteddfod of 1858 had a competition to compose a national anthem for Wales – a song on similar lines to *God Save The Queen* or *La Marseillaise* suggested the cleric and antiquarian John Williams (ab Ithel, 1811 - 1862) in a letter which appeared in *Yr Herald Cymraeg* of May 13, 1858. There were no entries. A prize was offered for an anthem at an Eisteddfod held in Carmarthen in the same year and although there was a winner, we know nothing of what became of the song. However, another competition at Llangollen provided what was evidently a much desired anthem.

It has been claimed that *Hen Wlad Fy Nhadau* was first sung in North Wales in an Eisteddfod on Christmas Day, 1859, in Seion Chapel, Cefn Mawr, near Wrexham. It was sung as a duet by Iolo Trefaldwyn and Seth Roberts of Brymbo with the audience joining in and repeating the chorus "with electrifying effect" according to what the minister, Dr Abel Jones Parry wrote in his autobiography *Hanner Canrif Llafur Gweinidogaethol* (Half a Century of Ministerial Labour). The Rev Eric Jones, minister of Yr Hen Dŷ Cwrdd Unitarian Chapel, Aberdare, told me that there is a note in the chapel records that *Hen Wlad Fy Nhadau* had been sung by a choir in four-part harmony accompanied by a string orchestra on New Year's Day, 1860. This would almost certainly be the first time for the anthem to be sung by a choir. "Hen Dŷ Cwrdd had a string orchestra, as did other chapels in Aberdare at the time.

And Llewelyn Alaw was a Unitarian and a prominent member of the chapel," said Eric Jones. The choir was conducted by Griffith Rhys Jones (Caradog), a virtuoso violinist, as well as leading the orchestra. Caradog was also a member of Hen Dŷ Cwrdd, although it has been said that he was not averse to joining chapels and churches of other denominations where congregations with good voices were to be found. Caradog went on to gain fame, if not exactly fortune, with his Great Choir winning the £1000 Challenge Cup at the Crystal Palace in 1872 and 1873. And when, in 1884, doubts were cast on the originality of the melody of *Hen Wlad Fy Nhadau* Caradog was among those who sprang to James James's defence.

The instant popularity of *Hen Wlad Fy Nhadau*, especially among the ordinary people, is remarkable. In spite of its secular nature it was sung as often in the chapels as in the taverns. Owain Alaw sang it as the climax of his concerts some time before he published it in his *Gems of Welsh Melody*. According to a report in *Yr Herald Cymraeg* (March 26, 1859) of a concert given by Owain Alaw in Caernarfon his performance of *Hen Wlad Fy Nhadau* was the highlight of the evening. D. G. Lloyd Hughes (*Y Faner*, August 3, 1984) wrote that *Hen Wlad Fy Nhadau* had been sung – along with *God Save The Queen* – at the end of an Eisteddfod in Llannerchymedd months after Owain Alaw's concert in Caernarfon.

Hen Wlad Fy Nhadau was an instant hit with ordinary Eisteddfod followers. It had a rousing chorus, easily learnt, and the crowds would join in with fervour. The great soloists of the day saw the audience response to the song and sang it themselves with gusto. It was sung by Owain Alaw and Llew Llwyfo (Lewis William Lewis) at the 1863 Rhyl Eisteddfod. The multi-talented Llew Llwyfo was a prolific poet, a journalist, novelist and a superb singer. At the Aberystwyth Eisteddfod of 1865 it was sung by Kate Wynne (sister of the famous Edith Wynne of Holywell) and in 1866 at Chester it was sung again by Llew Llwyfo. At the Chester Eisteddfod, according to the historian Dr John Davies, "*Hen Wlad Fy Nhadau* was sung with such passion that it was instantly adopted as the national anthem". It was sung at the end of every session of that Eisteddfod, and at every Eisteddfod from then on. The Eisteddfod was now evolving from relatively small events held in public houses frequented mostly by poets into much larger gatherings where music and large choirs were gaining ascendancy. *Hen Wlad Fy Nhadau* profited from, and was ideally suited to this new trend.

It was sung by Eos Morlais (Robert Rees, 1841-1892) at the 1873 Bangor National Eisteddfod. This was the same Eos who in the same year was the soloist when Caradog's Choir had its second success in the Crystal Palace and who stunned the audience with his rendition of *Annwyl yw Gwalia fy Ngwlad* (Dear is Wales my Country) after the result was announced. Eos Morlais was a talented musician and a sensational singer. Born in Dowlais, he had started work in a colliery at the age of nine, yet through his own efforts and aided by an uncle he educated himself. By 1870 he was acknowledged as "Wales's National Tenor". To be performed by Eos Morlais was the final stamp of approval for *Hen Wlad Fy Nhadau*. Among those listening to him that day in Bangor were Edith Wynne, Llew Llwyfo, James Sauvage, Brinley Richards (composer of *God Bless The Prince Of Wales*), Joseph Parry and Owain Alaw. According to the *Baner ac Amserau Cymru* reporter Eos Morlais's performance "had taken the Eisteddfod by storm". It was officially acknowledged as the Eisteddfod Song in Caernarfon in 1880 and sung at every Gorsedd ceremony after that.

Yet, as shown by D. G. Lloyd Hughes in *Y Faner* (August 3, 1984), there were those among the nation's leading lights who were uncomfortable with the song. Those tended, said Lloyd Hughes, "to put the English language and love of all things British ahead of Wales and the Welsh language. A patriotic song which fervently wished 'for the old language to endure' could expect a cool reception from such people."

He added: "Their aim was to find an eulogy to the Royal Family along the lines of God Save The Queen, to show everyone that the Welsh were second to none in their loyalty to the Crown. The response of the working classes gives cause to ask how deep in reality was that loyalty."

With *Hen Wlad Fy Nhadau* winning the hearts of the Welsh people a frantic race began to write something that would knock the song of the father and son from Pontypridd off its pedestal. John 'Ceiriog' Hughes wrote his poem '*I Wisgo Aur Goron*' to be sung to the jolly, and quite stirring, tune *Glan Medd-dod Mwyn* (The Verge of Sweet Intoxication) and won the support of John Roberts (Ieuan Gwyllt) the father of the *Cymanfa Ganu* (Hymn-singing Festival). Ceiriog was becoming paranoid in his attempts to write the words of a Welsh anthem. He wrote Welsh words to Brinley Richards's *God Bless The Prince of Wales*, which had been composed in 1862. That "sycophantic song" never caught on either – at least, not among the ordinary people. John Jones (Talhaiarn) also wrote words to be sung to *Glan Medd-dod Mwyn* but in a Wales where the temperance movement was taking hold, such sentiments as those expressed in the following couplet could not be expected to gain approval:

Ein gwydrau gorlenwn, mwyn yfwn mewn hedd,
O gwrw a gwirod, gwin, neithdar a medd

(Our glasses overflowing, let's all drink in peace
Of beer and liquour, wine, nectar and mead)

Talhaiarn desperately tried to compose something more temperate, but it was too late. What could he – and Ceiriog – have been thinking? An air to *sweet intoxication* for a Welsh National Anthem – it was preposterous! In any case, *Hen Wlad Fy Nhadau* had taken root in the hearts of the Welsh. Yet in spite of the song's popularity among the working classes and its acceptance among rank-and-file Eisteddfod followers, some of the Eisteddfod leaders were promoting Britishness and Englishness, said D. G. Lloyd Hughes, and hand-in-hand with them were Tories and Anglicans scared of radicalism and any talk of self-government. "… it could almost be said that there was a plot to frustrate the popularity of *Hen Wlad Fy Nhadau* by ignoring it," wrote Lloyd Hughes. It is even stranger to think that two of Wales's most popular 19th century poets, Ceiriog and Talhaiarn, tried so hard to write words that would be accepted as a National Anthem for Wales – and failed.

Hen Wlad Fy Nhadau was given a boost in a strange way at the London Eisteddfod of 1887, held at the Albert Hall. In the opinion of Hywel Teifi Edwards it was this that clinched it as far as getting the song accepted as Wales's National Anthem. Prince Albert Edward, Prince of Wales, eldest son of Queen Victoria, had for a quarter of a century managed to find excuses not to attend the National Eisteddfod. Now that it was held on his doorstep he could no longer keep away. Here again, Eos Morlais, the tenor from Dowlais, had a prominent part in the proceedings. In the session of August 12, he led the singing of *God Bless The Prince Of Wales* as the prince arrived. At the end of the session, Eos Morlais stood up again, this time to sing *Hen Wlad Fy Nhadau*. Albert and his family got up, too, and stood while the anthem was sung, with the usual fervour. Why he stood up, we may never know. Perhaps he thought he could – at last – go home. Maybe he thought Eos was about to sing a religious song – there was a time when an audience would stand for the *Hallelujah Chorus*. Whatever it was, he stood, and there could be no turning back. Royalty had given its seal of approval to Wales's National Anthem. There is a tale that a handsome copy of *Hen Wlad Fy Nhadau* was presented by a Lady Londonderry to Albert Edward in 1896, five years before he became king. That truth of that story may be uncovered one day, but not in time to be included here!

This was not the only occasion for Royalty to commend *Hen Wlad Fy Nhadau*. George V stopped at Pontypridd during a visit to South Wales on June 29, 1912 – he did not visit the town, merely alighting from the Royal Train to meet the local dignitaries on the platform. Luckily, Pontypridd station has the third longest island platform in Britain! Among those presented to him was Taliesin James. Taliesin, according to newspaper reports of the visit, presented him with a copy of the original version of the song, it's history and pictures of Evan and James all bound in *"velum and gold"*. According to the report the king later *"remarked to Lord Pontypridd that **Hen Wlad Fy** Nhadau was the finest song in the world."*

James, and some mysteries of the melody

James James, the eldest of Evan's children appears to have been his father's favourite. While Elizabeth James and the other children were attending Carmel Chapel, they were the two involved in music and poetry and rubbing shoulders with Myfyr Morganwg and the Druids at the Gorsedd of the Rocking Stone. James was born on December 4, 1832, in *Yr Hen Dafarn* (The Old Inn), Pontaberbargoed, in the same year as John "Ceiriog" Hughes, who was so anxious to write words for a Welsh anthem, and Islwyn, that fine poet from Gwent, who was born in nearby Sirhowey. James James was baptised at St Catwg's Church, Gelligaer, on April 12, 1833, and he was fifteen years old when the family moved to Pontypridd in 1847. He worked for a while with his father in the woollen factory in Mill Street. The woollen factory has long disappeared although many of the people of Pontypridd will remember the *County Hotel* that stood on the same site until it was demolished in the late 1950s. A plaque had been placed on the hotel wall in 1956, as part of the anthem's centenary celebrations, with the words in Welsh and English

Here lived Evan James 1809-1878 and his son James 1832-1902 when they composed in MDCCCLVI Hen Wlad Fy Nhadau

The site is now occupied by one of the departments of Rhondda-Cynon-Taf Council and the plaque visible to pedestrians crossing the Rhondda Bridge in the direction of Gelliwastad Road.

According to the Rev B. J. John's *Early History of the Rhondda Valley 1810 – 1910*, James, when he composed the melody of *Hen Wlad Fy Nhadau*, kept the *Welsh Harp* inn, which was sited about 100 yards up-river from the factory. A block of

The Colliers Arms Tavern in Mountain Ash, which was kept for many years by James James

flats at the bottom of Graigwen used to be known as the *Welsh Harp Buildings* and in the 1970s was the offices of the *Pontypridd Observer*. It seems that B. J. John may have been confused. The original *Welsh Harp* was a little closer to the river in the shadow of Brunel's railway bridge. On the other side of the road, almost opposite, was the *Colliers Arms*. The 1851 census shows that James was living with his parents in Tŷ'r Factory, Mill Street. Soon after, he married Cecilia, daughter of Morgan and Joan Miles, who were tenants of Gellifonaches farm. By 1856 he was probably living with his wife in a cottage attached to the *Colliers Arms*, working for his father and earning extra money as a pub harpist. In the 1861 census his occupation is given as a traveller and that he had two children, Taliesin aged four and Elizabeth who was one. We may assume that he was collecting orders for the factory. Soon after that he became a publican. His first inn was the *Walnut Tree Bridge*, Taff's Well. In 1873 he went to Mountain

Ash to keep the *Colliers Arms Tavern*, just off the Abercynon road – a convenient and popular place of refreshment for the men working at the *Deep Navigation* colliery. He was still at the *Colliers Arms* when the National Eisteddfod was held in Aberdare in 1885, and then in 1893, after the death of his wife Cecilia in 1893, he went to Aberaman to live in the *Swan* with his son Taliesin James (1857-1938). When he died in 1902, aged 70, he was living in Hawthorn Terrace, Aberdare. There is a family tradition that he died in his son's arms in the *Swan*. He was buried in the town's cemetery. As well as Taliesin, he had one other son and three daughters.

James, evidently, was an enthusiastic amateur musician. He had been taught to play the harp by a friend, the clock and cabinetmaker John Crockett of Taff Street, Pontypridd – the same John Crockett who became Taliesin James's first harp tutor, and probably the father of the John Crockett who was the recipient of the already quoted letter from Taliesin. The National Library of Wales has James James's personal songbook which includes popular songs he may have played in public houses, and religious music he may have sung in a choir – the *Hallelujah Chorus, Worthy Is The Lamb*, popular hymn tunes &c. It's a book that provides an interesting and useful insight into the kind of music that was popular in the South Wales industrial valleys. Some of the music he copied into his book contains only the tenor parts, so we can safely assume that he was a tenor. The book also includes what is generally accepted to be the original score of *Glan Rhondda* – or *Hen Wlad Fy Nhadau*. It appears on the same page as – below – *The Duke of York's March*; which may suggest that he did not rate his composition very highly. Or did he insert it later?

James composed his tune in the key of F – no problem for a tenor. It was the baritone Owain Alaw who transposed it to E Flat, making it easier for himself and more accessible for large crowds of rugby supporters and Eisteddfod audiences.

Such has been the interest in the story – indeed, the mystery – surrounding the composition of *Hen Wlad Fy Nhadau* that there have been conflicting stories, even from those purporting to be quoting Taliesin James. In the *Western Mail* of September 11, 1930, Lewis Davies (Lewys Glyn Cynon) tells his readers how Taliesin James repeated to him how his father – James James – had told him many times how he had "conceived a melody" while walking along the Rhondda road inspired by the "...rippling of the river which flowed close by ..." on a Sunday **morning** in January 1856. In his letter to John Crockett Taliesin was saying it was composed in the **afternoon**. Owen Morgan (Morien) gives his own flowery version in his *History of Pontypridd and Rhondda Valleys* while we get a slightly different story again from Sir Alfred T. Davies in his pamphlet *The Story of the National Anthem of Wales*, published on the occasion of the unveiling of the plaque in the Glyn Ceiriog Memorial Institute in 1943. (See Appendices 2 and 3.) It is ironic that the village of Glyn Ceiriog chose to make this declaration of thanks to the father and son from Pontypridd for their *gift* to the nation. John 'Ceiriog' Hughes, so desperate to supplant *Hen Wlad Fy Nhadau* as Wales's anthem with words of his own, was born in Llanarmon, the neighbouring village up the Ceiriog valley.

We can at least be certain that James had intended the song to be sung in the key of F. But did he have other intentions? There is a tradition in Pontypridd, emanating from Mrs Mona Gray who owned the White Palace Cinema in Pontypridd (now a Bingo Hall) that the song used to be sung much livelier than the way we sing it today – more like a jig. Mrs Gray was the daughter of Mrs E. C. Parfitt who has already been mentioned, and she, in turn, was the daughter of

Elizabeth John who first sang *Hen Wlad Fy Nhadau* in Tabor Vestry, Maesteg. An ITV Wales programme broadcast in November 2005, *Land of my Father*, presented by the writer and broadcaster Trevor Fishlock sought the opinion of the composer Gareth Glyn. Mr Glyn described it as a "harpist's song" – a song easily played on the harp – and said it had many characteristics of a jig. To illustrate the point he played it on the piano as a jig in $6/8$ time. He showed it to be a pretty and attractive tune – although it is hard to imagine it being sung with such haste today.

It has already been noted that Llewelyn Alaw was not the only person to submit an entry for a collection of unpublished melodies in the 1858 Llangollen Eisteddfod; there were two others. The one that interests us is that submitted under the *nom de plume* of Orpheus and was awarded a special prize of £5 on the recommendation of the adjudicator Owain Alaw. *Glan Rhondda* was included in Orpheus's collection, too. This could have been because the song was already popular, at least in and around Pontypridd, and that Orpheus lived in the area. As the Leeds musician Percy A. Scholes wrote in his article *Hen Wlad Fy Nhadau* (*National Library of Wales Journal*, Summer 1943), Orpheus's version is quite different to the melody in James James's private songbook and to the version (NLW 331) in the Llewelyn Alaw collection. Orpheus's version being, in Scholes's opinion, the result of an imperfect recollection based on having heard the song once. Interestingly, when we recall local tradition in Pontypridd, Orpheus's version is set in $6/8$ time, not in $3/4$. Many, including Percy Scholes and Tecwyn Ellis (*National Library of Wales Journal*, 1954) have noted that the tune is musically more correct in $6/8$ time. Also, the word *vivace* (lively) is the instruction written above Orpheus's *Glan Rhondda*. Interestingly, the four first lines of Orpheus's version have been arranged – albeit a very basic arrangement – for two voices, and the chorus for four voices.

Dr Meredydd Evans and his wife, Phyllis Kinney, recently offered a startling theory to anyone interested in the history of *Hen Wlad Fy Nhadau*, namely that James James himself was Orpheus. In a fascinating article that appeared in the periodical *Hanes Cerddoriaeth Cymru/History of Welsh Music* (Vol 5, 2002) Dr Evans goes in pursuit of the story of the Orpheus manuscript. In spite of Owain Alaw's praise and his exhortation that the collection should be safeguarded, it appears to have disappeared for a number of years. It was eventually found by a commercial traveller named Lewis Hartley, probably in a second-hand bookshop, who bought it for a few pence. He had it bound in beautiful red leather and in 1888 gave it as a wedding present to W. Cadwaladr Davies, then registrar of the University College, Bangor, a man who played a prominent role in establishing higher education in Wales. He later became a barrister in London and his wife-to-be, Mary Davies, was also well known in London Welsh circles. Mary Davies (1855-1930) was a professional singer, and held in high regard in London Welsh and Eisteddfodic circles. Her father was the musician and sculptor from Merthyr, William Davies (Mynorydd). Cadwaladr Davies died in 1905, and after a few months had elapsed, Mary Davies sent the Orpheus collection to John Lloyd Williams, a collector of folk music and eventually editor of *Cylchgrawn Cymdeithas Alawon Gwerin Cymru* (Journal of the Welsh Folk Song Society). She did this, says Meredydd Evans, without fully realising the significance of the manuscript. Lloyd Williams in no time at all was making good use of it. "Of the 25 songs published in the first issue of the Journal in 1909, ten came from Orpheus's collection," writes Dr Evans.

John Lloyd Williams set about trying to discover the

identity of Orpheus. In an entry dated July 18, 1910, he wrote "Discov'd that the compiler of the Llangollen 1858 MS was James James, Composer of Hen Wlad Fy Nhadau" and again on the same date "All day at Brit Mus ... Discovered that the compiler of Mrs Davies's 1858 Collection was, in all probability Composer Yr Hen Wlad Fy Nhadau". (Cited by Dr Meredydd Evans.) Yet, although his private papers suggest absolute certainty, he did not go public with his theory. Dr Evans believes this was because Lloyd Williams had seen a letter from Taliesin James to Mary Davies insisting that his father had not sent a collection of songs to the 1858 Llangollen Eisteddfod competition. He wrote: "... I have not the slightest doubt in my mind but that Mr T. D. Llewelyn (Llewelyn Alaw) was the sender of both collections, for I am certain my father did not give his song to anyone but Mr Llewelyn, and I am equally certain my father did not enter the competition himself."

We can be fairly certain that James – or Evan – had given copies of the song to others. Taliesin James, himself, in the John Crockett letter, describes the children of Pontypridd singing and whistling the tune as they went around the town. We recall the story of Evan giving a copy to Elizabeth John to give to Miss Miles. There are other reasons for doubting Taliesin James's testimony. There is in Pontypridd Library a letter, dated June 1, 1911, from Taliesin written to a cousin – it begins *Dear Cousin* – asking for all kinds of fairly basic information, e.g. the dates of birth and death of his grandfather, his grandmother's name, his father's date and place of birth &c. Mrs Barbara Jenkins suggests that the cousin was another Taliesin James. He should be expected to have this kind of information at his finger-tips, especially as he makes some very confident assertions on other, more complex, questions. Lewis Davies in the *Western Mail* quotes Taliesin as saying that James composed the melody on a Sunday **morning** when recovering from rheumatic fever, a quite serious illness. In his letter to John Crockett he says the tune was composed on a Sunday **afternoon** and there is no mention of an illness. I read somewhere else that it was Evan James who was recuperating from illness. And there is, of course, the controversy as to whether it was the tune or the words that came first.

Dr Meredydd Evans also cites an article discovered by John Lloyd Williams in *Cerddor y Cymry* (The Welsh Musician), edited by W. T. Rees (Alaw Ddu). Rees, born in Pwllyglaw near Port Talbot, and whose family then moved to Aberdare, and he himself later lived in Rhondda and Pontypridd, evidently knew Evan and James well and was almost certainly on friendly terms with them. W. T. Rees wrote: "We remember the fluency of the old poet as he told us how his son composed the music, and how it was sent to a competition for a collection of Welsh melodies to an Eisteddfod in North Wales, and how the adjudicator, Owain Alaw, liked it so much that he arranged it for his *Gems of Welsh Melodies* and how it came to be generally admired through his efforts in performing it in his concerts."

John Lloyd Williams considered this to be significant statement in his quest to identify James James as Orpheus. Of course, the sentence is not an unequivocal statement that **James James** sent the song to the Llangollen Eisteddfod – we know that Llewelyn Alaw sent it the same Eisteddfod in his collection, too. But by taking the sentence in its context, Dr Meredydd Evans told me that he also saw this as a significant sentence. What puts the identity of Orpheus beyond question, says Meredydd Evans, is the handwriting. This is what Dr Evans wrote in *History of Welsh Music*:

"On February 18, 1998, I happened to visit the National Library's Permanent Exhibition. I saw James James 'Song Book' and it was open on the page that contains Glan Rhondda. My attention was riveted in particular by the notation. I thought I recognised the handwriting. I immediately arranged to compare the 'Song Book' with the handwriting of 'Orpheus' and I had no doubt but that the same hand was responsible for both. Later, I asked Daniel Huws, who is a palaeographer of distinction, to compare the book and the handwriting. He also did that, which is why I can say with hand on heart that James James was, and is, 'Orpheus'. "

I discussed this with Mr Daniel Huws, a former Head of the Manuscripts Department of the National Library, and he told me that after Dr Meredydd Evans had made the connection and noticed the similarity in the handwriting it was a small matter to confirm and prove that Orpheus was James James.

This settles the argument as to how James intended his song to be sung. Especially as he inserted the instruction *Vivace* on the copy he sent to Llangollen under the *nom de plume* of Orpheus. This shows there were three early versions of *Hen Wlad Fy Nhadau* – four when we count *Glan y Rhondda*, which, in Dr Meredydd Evans's opinion, was also included in Llewelyn Alaw's collection. We have the version in James's 'Song Book'; the one we know for certain – and possibly another – in Llewelyn Alaw's collection; and the one from James James's own collection submitted under the name of Orpheus. This suggests that Llewelyn Alaw's version – not that of Orpheus – is the *"product of imperfect memory (perhaps the hearing of one performance)"* in the words of Percy Scholes. Scholes writes of the Orpheus version:

It is in 6/8 time, two bars being thrown into one throughout, and metrically is the most correct of all the versions ...

Dr Meredydd Evans and Phyllis Kinney's belief that two versions of Glan Rhondda were included in Llewelyn Alaw's collection, *Glan Rhondda* (NLW 331) and *Glan y Rhondda* (NLW 129B) is significant. Did Llewelyn, as Taliesin James's letter suggests, jot down the notes "*sitting on a three-legged stool*" as James sang it to him "*from the loom*"? Llewelyn was undoubtedly a fine musician, yet if he had had to jot down the melody in a hurry, did he have difficulty in deciphering his notes and had included two versions in his collection? *Glan y Rhondda* is basically the same tune but with differences from the other versions, and although interesting in its own right it is difficult to come to any conclusion other than that Llewelyn Alaw had had difficulty in reading his own notation.

This begs another question. Did James James set out to mislead us by inserting a more "recent" version of *Glan Rhondda* in his '*Song Book*', the one picked out of Llewelyn Alaw's collection and popularised by Owain Alaw? The songs in James's songbook consist of compositions and songs noted down for his own use in a period extending from 1849 to 1863. *Glan Rhondda* appears on the same page as – and below – *The Duke of York's March*. There may be a number of reasons for this. Perhaps, as has been suggested, he did not rate the song very highly when he composed it. Somehow, this does not ring true, especially in view of the apparent enthusiasm surrounding the song's birth. We have to accept that two years later he included a different version of *Glan Rhondda* in a collection of songs he was submitting to a competition in the 1858 Llangollen Eisteddfod. We can only assume James James was including the version that was his composition and the version, presumably, he had been singing and accompanying in pubs and Eisteddfodau in and around Pontypridd. How, then, do we explain the version we find in James's 'Song Book'? Did he believe, in view of events following the Llangollen Eisteddfod, that the song he had composed was in danger of flying away from him and that it now owed more than he would care to acknowledge to Llewelyn Alaw's version of it – or at least, one of Llewelyn's versions? Did he feel he was losing control of the music he had composed and inserted a version of it in his personal 'Song Book', sometime after 1858, as proof of ownership or for the "benefit" of future researchers? A version much closer to how it was being sung in concerts all over North Wales by Owain Alaw. The fact that he inserts the words "Composed January 1856" above the copy is no proof that he actually wrote that version down in the book at the time he composed it.

I find it surprising, too, that he does not give an actual date for the composition; the January 6th, 1856, date is one that has been suggested by Mrs Barbara Jenkins, and could well be correct. But the omission of a more precise date by James James is strange. There are other questions, which will never be answered satisfactorily. Taliesin James, in his letter to John Crockett, writes that Llewelyn Alaw came to the factory and asked his father whether he knew of any unpublished songs. "My father replied saying he did not..." says Taliesin. He then goes on to say that James mentioned Glan Rhondda and offered to sing it to him. Either James was saying that he did not know any traditional songs, which is very unlikely; or, and this would seem far more likely, he intended competing himself and was not going to share his songs with another competitor. He would have nothing to lose by offering his own song – and, as it turned out, he might have a lot to gain. And by insisting that his father was not Orpheus, was Taliesin – as Dr

Meredydd Evans suggested to me – trying to conceal that his father had come off second best in the Llangollen Eisteddfod competition? Or he may be wishing to conceal a more embarrassing secret, that *Hen Wlad Fy Nhadau* as it was now being sung was a much-changed version of his father's original composition. It could explain why the identity of Orpheus was concealed for so long, James may not have wished it to be known that his own version was quite different from the song that was gathering impetus as Wales's national song.

The Orpheus collection contains traditional melodies as well as – in Meredydd Evans's opinion – other songs composed by James James. The collection also contains four songs attributed to Thomas James of the Llanover Inn, Pontypridd, also referred to as T. ab Iago, and we find the name Dewi ab Iago under another song. We know that Evan James had two brothers who were poets, Thomas (who also called himself Tomos ab Iago) and David (who called himself Dewi ab Iago). A few poems by both of them can be found among the Evan James MSS in The National Library.

Accepting that James James was Orpheus, this adds an interesting dimension to the picture we have of him – even if it does detract something from his role as the composer of the anthem. "He was obviously a man of vision," Mr Daniel Huws told me. "Earlier in the century there had been attempts at collecting Welsh folk melodies – notably the famous collection of Maria Jane Williams, Aberpergwm. But by the middle of the 19th century the Welsh were becoming 'respectable' and turning their backs on traditional folk music, and there were hardly any collectors. Llewelyn Alaw was one of the few. So the fact that were was another working class man in the industrial southeast with the vision to collect folk tunes was important and significant. We did not have a collector of importance until John Lloyd Williams emerged at the beginning of the 20th century." As has already been noted, Lloyd Williams made good use of the Orpheus collection.

Then, in 1884, a bitter note of controversy entered the story of *Hen Wlad Fy Nhadau*. A letter by a Frederick Atkins, organist at St John's Church in the centre of Cardiff, appeared in the March 8 edition of the *South Wales Daily News*:

" ... before it gets handed down to posterity as a Welsh air, permit me to point out that it (Land of my Fathers) is taken note for note almost from one in an old English comic opera ... The air is known as 'Tiptin o' Rosin the Beau', and is to be found in some old books – notably instruction books."

James James responded by telling how the song had been included in Llewelyn Alaw's winning collection in the Llangollen Eisteddfod, and how Owain Alaw included it in his *Gems of Welsh Melodies*. He added: "I know nothing whatever of the melody named by Mr Atkins."

Passions were aroused in the letters pages of the *South Wales Daily News* and the *Western Mail* over the next couple of months. Although quick with his condemnation it soon became apparent that Atkins was unable to find a copy of the song from the "*old English comic opera*". When the *Western Mail* tried to get copies a strange story emerged that there had been fires at the publisher's warehouses and every copy destroyed! "... extraordinary to relate, both the music warehouses in Paternoster-row to which we had given orders were burnt down on the every evening their parcels were to be dispatched." Atkins offered to provide a copy from memory for the *Western Mail*, an offer the paper initially declined as he could have been open to accusations of distorting the tune in support of his assertion. Something at least one letter writer from Mountain Ash accused him of doing! "It ... behoves the public to be on its guard accepting, as genuine, Mr Atkins's arrangement of the air ..."

Glan Rhondda as it appears in James James's personal songbook

The version of Tiptin o' Rosin the Beau from Musical Bouquet. The two tunes appeared in the Cardiff Times and South Wales Weekly News (April 12, 1884) above a letter from a Mr R. H. Jones, Maesycwmmer (see below)

It is hard to understand why it was so difficult to get a copy of the song as it had been published in an edition of the journal *Musical Bouquet*, in 1856! It then emerged that many of the letter writers were familiar with *Tiptin o' Rosin the Beau*, that there were many versions of the tune, and it became a matter of debate as to which one was correct. (Phyllis Kinney told me that she knew of at least four, only one of which in any way at all resembles *Hen Wlad Fy Nhadau*.) A letter writer in the *South Wales Daily News* (April 28, 1884) said of *Tiptin o' Rosin the Beau* that "... it was an old Scottish favourite with a new face, very slightly altered, and well known far and wide as *I lo'e na laddie but ane ...*" A sketchy picture of the arguments together with extracts from various letters were included in an article by Tecwyn Ellis, who became Director of Education for Meirionnydd, in the *National Library of Wales Journal* (1954) where he arrives at the – rather odd – conclusion:

"There is little doubt that *Hen Wlad Fy Nhadau* as we know it today, has been adapted from the air *Rosin the Beau*, but Wales has not accepted the unpleasant truth."

It is impossible to see exactly how Tecwyn Ellis came to his conclusion as his extracts are short and are of the sweeping statements variety without including the more detailed analysis. He also mentions in passing matters about which more information would be interesting and perhaps relevant. For instance, he acknowledges having seen a copy of *I lo'e na laddie but ane* by someone in Corwen, but does not say whether it is, in his opinion, the same song or one very similar to, *Tiptin o' Rosin the Beau*. In his article Ellis includes a version of *Tiptin o' Rosin the Beau* provided by the *English Folk Dance and Song Society* which is quite different to that published in the *Musical Bouquet*. He includes a very brief extract from a letter by R. H. Jones of Maesycwmmer that appeared in the *Cardiff Times and South Wales Weekly News* (April 12, 1884), "*the first and fairest of James's supporters*". But his extract from this "fair" letter is exceedingly short. Here is a fairly long extract from it. After rebuking the editor for errors in the score of *Hen Wlad Fy Nhadau*, printed in the previous edition and asking for these to be corrected R. H. Jones continues:

"This will give you a correct copy of the original *Hen Wlad Fy Nhadau* which I have been allowed to examine by the author, Mr James James of Mountain Ash. I will now proceed to analyse both melodies and would ask your readers to observe in starting that the phrases of *Rosin the Beau* consist of two bars each, in six-eight time, whilst the phrases of *Hen Wlad Fy Nhadau* consist of four bars each, in three-four time. In referring to the first two bars of *Rosin the Beau* and the first four bars of *Hen Wlad Fy Nhadau* it does not appear to me possible for even the most fertile imagination to establish the slightest similarity. Take the second phrase in *Rosin the Beau* and the next four bars, or the second phrase of *Hen Wlad Fy Nhadau* omitting the first 3 notes. I am sure your musical readers will at once admit that it would be useless to search for any comparison, and I submit that the three notes which I have referred to are totally valueless from a melodic point of view. We will now proceed to the third phrase in *Rosin the Beau* which is identical with the first, and compare it with the third phrase in the Welsh air, and I venture to assert that there is not the slightest typical identity discoverable; the first and third phrases in *Rosin the Beau* are precisely the same, whilst in *Hen Wlad Fy Nhadau* we have a different phrase altogether. In the fourth phrase of 'Rosin the Beau' and in the corresponding phrase of *Hen Wlad Fy Nhadau* I willingly admit that it is quite apparent to the most superficial observer that there is no difficulty in discerning a very striking and reasonable similarity, but your musical students will at once observe that this similarity is easily accounted for, being the first full and authentic cadence which must progress from dominant to tonic. I would invite your readers' special attention to the next, or fifth phrase of *Rosin the Beau*, as printed by you today, and ask them to compare it with the same phrase as it appeared in your issue of the 8th inst. In that copy, written by Mr Atkins, this phrase has been so manipulated that it bears a most striking similarity to *Hen Wlad Fy Nhadau*, but will my friend Mr Atkins allow me to ask him upon what authority he writes the phrase in this manner? Is it not possible that Mr Atkins has had this strain from *Hen Wlad Fy Nhadau* echoing in the corners of his memory? Until I have more substantial evidence than Mr Atkins's recollections of Mrs Fitzwilliam's charming singing flitting through his mind, I have no alternative but to acquit Mr James of anything approaching plagiarism – even unintentionally – on this score. Neither the copy which you print today nor the one which appeared as a supplement to the *Western Mail* on the 7th inst would justify Mr Atkins's score. Both my copies – if I might call them such – are here identical, excepting the grace notes, which further estrange *Hen Wlad Fy Nhadau* from *Rosin the Beau*, and both differ from Mr Atkins's copy. The sixth phrase of *Rosin the Beau* is identical with the second, both ending alike, which endings differ in *Hen Wlad Fy Nhadau*, both phrases in *Rosin the Beau*, terminating on the sixth of the key, as a third to the harmony of the sub-dominant, but in *Hen Wlad Fy Nhadau* it is not so.

"We will next compare the seventh phrases of both airs. The reader will here observe that this phrase is identical with the 1st and 3rd in *Rosin the Beau* as printed by you today, which are, as we have pointed out, totally dissimilar to the corresponding phrases or to the seventh phrase in *Hen Wlad Fy Nhadau*, which as your readers will see is a repetition of the third phrase of the same air, whereas in Mr Atkins's copy, he makes his seventh phrase a repetition of his fifth, and here again it serves the same purpose, being a repetition which is so manipulated as to correspond with the repeat in *Hen Wlad Fy Nhadau*, which process estranges Mr Atkins's score from the only two copies of *Rosin the Beau* which I have been able to put my hands upon. The eighth phrase is a repetition of the fourth in *Rosin the Beau* and the infinitesimal similarity found between the structure of the two melodies here must be repeated as the only full and authentic cadences."

It is obvious, apart from the phrase "*Tros ryddid gollasant eu gwaed*" and echoed in "*O bydded i'r heniaith barhau*" that there is no other similarity in the two tunes. I have compared *Rosin the Beau* from the two copies I have seen with *Hen Wlad Fy Nhadau* as adapted to a jig played in 6/8 time by Mr Gareth Glyn for the television programme *Land of My Father* and again I could see no similarity except for the final phrase. I think it reasonable, also, to expect a musician of the quality and reputation of Owain Alaw to have noticed any similarities when he first found *Glan Rhondda* in Llewelyn Alaw's collection and certainly before he included it in his *Gems of Welsh Melodies*.

"It appears that *Rosin the Beau* was an old Irish dance tune that became popular as a song in the 19th century," says Ms Kinney (cited by W. Rhys Nicholas). (Mr Tim Saunders has told me that an Irish republican song known as *The Boys of Kilmichael* was also sung to the tune *Rosin the Beau*.) "There is not much difference in the various airs of this tune as it appeared in different countries. There is a variant of *Rosin the Beau* noted by Mrs Evans, Whitchurch, which is almost identical with the one noted in the United States. But if you compare these with *Hen Wlad Fy Nhadau* the differences are significant, although the two airs are similar in 'shape' the harmonic cadences are different. On the whole there is only one musical phrase which is identical in both tunes, the phrase on the words 'Tros ryddid gollasant eu gwaed', which is repeated at the end in the words 'O bydded i'r heniaith barhau'. There is a similarity, but in my opinion *Hen Wlad Fy Nhadau* is not a variant of *Rosin the Beau*. It is more probable that the musical phrases of *Rosin the Beau* were familiar generally because of the popularity of Irish airs in the 19th century, and that James James was familiar with them. But it is a long way from saying that a composer was influenced unknowingly by a piece of music and saying that one composition was a copy of another."

I discussed the matter further with Dr Meredydd Evans and Phyllis Kinney.

Dr Evans stressed the importance of comparing melodies scientifically and that the occasional echo was not enough evidence to claim that one song is a copy of another. "The art of comparative musical study developed a lot during the 20th century," he said. "Such a thing exists as 'families' of airs and just because two melodies even belong to the same 'family' is no proof that one has taken anything from another. We must look at the general form of the song and the form of the melody in particular. The music must draw together as an entity – the form and spirit of the song must be similar before we can even talk of plagiarism. Echoing is a frequent and inevitable occurrence in music, and there are insufficient similarities to justify the accusations of plagiarism made against James James. Nor should we forget the English mindset of the period, either – that nothing good ever came out of Wales."

The point about the "English mindset" was relevant when we recall the period. Evan James made an oblique reference to it in a speech delivered at the Gelligaer Eisteddfod six years before *Hen Wlad Fy Nhadau* was composed. This will be discussed later (see page 111 and Appendix 4). In the debate about the originality of the music of *Hen Wlad Fy Nhadau*, the views of the participants often reflected their political point of view – Liberal home-rulers against English nationalists. It is not difficult in this period to find hostility to all things Welsh among English historians, archaeologists, folk studies experts &c. Note how Frederick Atkins instantly claimed *Old Rosin the Beau* to be an **English** air! It soon became clear that it was a very old Scottish tune, with the Irish, too, laying claim to it.

The whole unpleasant controversy has long been forgotten. So how did the argument arise? English jealousy at seeing such a dignified anthem stirring the people of their tiny next-door neighbour? The debate was ignored by Percy Scholes in his article on *Hen Wlad Fy Nhadau* in *The National Library of Wales Journal* (Summer, 1943). Why did Tecwyn Ellis pursue the story and how did he arrive at his strange conclusion? *"We all nod off at times,"* Meredydd Evans suggested to me. I recall, in the Fifties, a move to try to replace *Hen Wlad Fy Nhadau* as the Welsh national anthem with Elfed's hymn *Cofia'n Gwlad* (Remember our Country). The hymn-writer and poet, 'Elfed' Lewis was probably thinking more of Britain than of Wales when he wrote his fine hymn. But the secularism of Evan James's words has, from time to time, been the cause of some concern to the more religious among the Welsh people. Did Tecwyn Ellis, perhaps, have sympathies with those concerns?

James James's name will forever be linked to one of the world's great anthems – even if changes have been made to it on its way to popularity and acceptance. A comparison of Madge Breeze's 1899 recording with the way it is sung today shows how the song has changed over the last hundred years. Indeed, in view of the revelations of Dr Meredydd Evans – supported by Mr Daniel Huws – it is becoming clear that others, even the Welsh nation in its entirety, made some contribution to the present form of *Hen Wlad Fy Nhadau*, in particular to its tempo and how it is sung. That the letter by that man Atkins stirred up such a furious response, with musicians of the reputation of Caradog rushing to James James's defence is proof that by 1884 *Hen Wlad Fy Nhadau* had won the hearts of a nation.

Let another Englishman have the last word on this debate, the wise and balanced Percy Scholes (cited by Oswald Edwards):

"It will be known to most readers that complete originality is an impossibility. Every piece of music, big or little, however "original" it may be in it's general effect contains far and away more un-original material than original – so much so that it is often pretty hard to determine to what the general effect of originality is due. Any student of folk tunes knows that the same melodic phrases crop up again and again in different tunes."

On this occasion, Dr Scholes's subject was not *Hen Wlad Fy Nhadau*. He was writing a defence of an old French tune with characteristics taken from a number of other airs – *God Save The King/Queen*!

The James's family

Evan James (Ieuan ab Iago), author of the words of *Hen Wlad Fy Nhadau*, was the son of another Evan James. Evan James, the father, was born in the Parish of Eglwysilan on August 29, 1773. Eglwysilan, along with Llanwynno, Llanfabon and Penycoedcae is one of the ancient hilltop villages surrounding the new town of Pontypridd, and is sited on the crest of the mountain between Pontypridd and Abertridwr. He, too, was the son of a weaver who had established a woollen mill in Caerphilly in 1750 who, it is suggested, may have come from Cardiganshire. The old Evan James married Elizabeth Stradling of Caerphilly in 1791. There is a family tradition that Elizabeth Stradling was descended from the celebrated Stradlings of St Donat's – Taliesin James, or his cousin of the same name, appears to have been the source of that information. This branch of the Stradling family, originally from Switzerland, had been settled in Wales since at least the 14th. Over the centuries the family had amassed a fine library and were the proud patrons of poets and Welsh culture.

The brilliant period of this noble family ended when the heir, Sir Thomas Stradling, was killed in a duel in Montpellier on September 27, 1738. Thomas Stradling had gone on the "European tour", in the manner of wealthy young men, with a friend from his university days name of John Tyrwhitt. It seems that they entered into a pact – should one of them die during the journey, the other would inherit his estate. The tradition in the Stradling family is that one evening Tyrwhitt plied Sir Thomas with drink, accused him of insulting behaviour, challenged him to a duel and killed him. After Sir Thomas's body had been brought back St Donat's, Tyrwhitt turned up with the piece of paper signed by the deceased testifying to the pact they had made. In 1755, after years of litigation, the Stradling heirs were forced to leave what remained of the St Donat's family estate.

According to G. T. Clarke's genealogy of the families of Glamorgan (*Limbus Patrum Morganiae et Glamorganiae*, 1886) the estate was divided into three parts and he gives details of branches of the family settling in a number of places including Roath (Cardiff), Llantwit Major, Merthyr Mawr, Kenfig and Gelligaer. Not that this is of great significance, but there was an Elizabeth Stradling (neé Mansell) in an earlier generation who had married into the family. It would not have been possible that the Elizabeth Stradling who married Evan James – even if she was a direct descendent of the family – to have ever spent any part of her childhood in St Donat's Castle. But who knows, she may have taken pride in her ancestors' role as patrons of Welsh poets and poetry and that she and her husband had passed on some of that culture to the children, amongst them Evan (Ieuan ab Iago), author of the words of *Hen Wlad Fy Nhadau*.

Evan and Elizabeth James had 14 children, three of whom did not survive infancy. The records show the family was living in the Parish of Eglwysilan when most of the children were born. At that time Eglwysilan parish was very large. The river Taff was its western boundary along which it extended from Whitchurch in the south to Cilfynydd in the north. The river Rhymni formed its eastern boundary, extending from Ystrad Mynach in the north to Cefn Onn (Caerphilly). The Parish of Caerphilly was not separated from that of Eglwysilan until 1850. When Evan James, author of *Hen Wlad Fy Nhadau*, was born in 1809, it appears that the family lived in a cottage, named Bryngolau, 11 Castle Street, which was attached to the Castle Inn, Caerphilly. The Workmen's Hall now occupies the site. In the 1851 Census for Pontypridd,

Caerphilly is noted as his place of birth. The children were brought up in the Christian tradition and Evan James – the father – had been, according to his son's poems, a Sunday School teacher throughout his life. He continued with his occupation as a weaver and a picture emerges of a person held in high esteem within the community – after all, he owned his woollen mill and factory and was married to a Stradling. By 1813 the family had moved to the Ancient Druid Inn, on the outskirts of Hollybush, Argoed, in the Parish of Bedwellty. The buildings are still occupied, the little cottages still charming, and the building, which may have been a woollen mill, a pub – or both – is also occupied. They are buildings wonderfully sited over-looking a wooded valley. When Evan James and Elizabeth went back to Caerphilly to bury their five-week-old baby, James, in St Martin's Church on March 22, 1814, Evan is described as being Mayor of Bedwellty. Another boy, born later, was also named James – this was the one who eventually emigrated and may well have been the writer of the letter urging Evan James, the son, to come to America, thus inspiring a response in the form of a poem that was to become the Welsh national anthem.

Evan James (Ieuan ab Iago), born in 1809, was the tenth of the 14 children. According to Thomas T. Leyshon, and Daniel Huws makes a similar suggestion, Elizabeth (neé Stradling) James died after the birth of the last of the children, around 1816. But the researches of another of the family's descendents, Mrs Barbara Jenkins, indicate that she was almost certainly buried in 1824. An entry in a family Bible shows she was buried in St Martin's Church, Caerphilly, and the most likely date, from the Church Register, would make it seem that she died on December 3, 1824, and that she was buried on December 12. In fact, this is the date given by Mr Leyshon in the family tree although, in the text, he gives the year of her death as 1816. Evan James, the father, remarried another woman named Elizabeth – Elizabeth Williams, a widow from Merthyr Tydfil, who was a year older than him in St Catwg's Church, Gelligaer, on December 22, 1826, in *"the presence of William Pritchard and William Phillips"*. Evan James and his second wife were both into their fifties by the time they married and there were certainly no children from this marriage. Did Evan marry a maid who had taken a prominent part in raising the family? After all, eleven children was quite a number of children to rear, not counting the three who died in infancy. The family had evidently moved to Argoed around 1816, yet when Evan – the son – recalls his childhood in his poetry years later, it is the time he spent on the small farm of Ffos yr Hebog, up in the hills on Gelligaer common, a mile northeast of the village of Deri, that inspires his muse:

> *Rhaeadr Nant Bargoed gogyfer a'r crofft*
> *A'm suodd i ganwaith i gysgu.*

> (It was the Bargoed Brook alongside the croft
> That sang me a hundred times to sleep.)

Nant Bargoed does not flow near Ffos yr Hebog, so Evan was probably taking poetic licence and describing Nant Bargoed down in the valley, near where the brook flows into the Rhymni river, by *Yr Hen Dafarn*. This became known later as the *Old Mill Inn*; was rebuilt as the *Old Mill Hotel* and is now known as *The Gold Mine*, although the name *Old Mill Hotel* can still be seen on the gable end wall. The stream would have passed by the factory, and the inn. The factory was owned by his older brother Edward and his wife Mary while the inn was kept by his sister Mary and her husband, Thomas Lewis.

Naturally, he may have spent time at the homes of his older brother and sister. He writes affectionately, too, of his upbringing in these parts:

... dan ofal gwyliadwrus
Fy llysfam fwyn a'm tad.

(... under the watchful care
of my gentle stepmother and father.)

This poem may have misled people to believe that his father had re-married. In another poem – *Y Sycamorwydden yn Ymyl y Nant* (The Sycamore at the Edge of the Brook) that again appears to be set down in the valley – he writes of his early education:

... addysg yn foreu er fy rhinweddoli
Tan nawdd fy nhad a fy mam.

(early education for my moral good
under the care of my father and mother.)

Ffos yr Hebog – Hawk's Ditch does no justice to the beauty of the Welsh name – where he spent years of his youth was a typical Welsh long house. The house, although retaining some of its original interior features, has been changed by extensions. The moorland farm is now the headquarters of a bus company, with double-deckers and garages dwarfing the house. Thomas Leyshon writes that the family were not there for long and that they moved to the village of Nelson in 1820.

If so, they would have moved there before the mother's death, although Mr Leyshon insists otherwise. The family retained ownership of the farm for quite some time afterwards. There is agreement that in 1837 Evan James, the father who had by now remarried, moved to Pant y Trwyn, near Ynys-ddu, in the Parish of Mynydd Islwyn. Evan, the son, confirms this with a series of *englynion* – four line poems in traditional Welsh metre – wishing his "parents" well in their new home, written on the "shortest day", 1837. He refers to them as father and mother, not – accurately – father and stepmother. Evan's poems are not always reliable guides to historical detail!

The old Evan James died in 1856, the year *Hen Wlad Fy Nhadau* was composed, and he was buried at St Catwg's Church, Gelligaer. He spent his last years within easy distance of his son's family, a tenant of the Hafod Estate, living at Troed Rhiw Trwyn, one of the oldest farmhouses in the Rhondda. Troed Rhiw Trwyn, a charmingly maintained listed building, is sited off the old road from Hopkinstown to Llwyncelyn where visitors are assured of a welcome from the present owner. Elizabeth James outlived her husband by six years, and died at the age of 90.

Of the children at least three were weavers with their own mills and factories – Edward, David (Dewi ab Iago) and Evan (Ieuan ab Iago). During the 19th century the family had expanded their activities and sphere of influence in the production of cloth and flannel in the south-eastern valleys. Edward James and his wife Mary owned the factory at Aberbargoed while Evan and his wife, Elizabeth (another Elizabeth – she was a Jones before she married), owned a factory at Argoed and eventually rented the one at Pontypridd. The last of the family's factories to survive was that of Morgan James, on the banks of the Rhymni below the Maesycwmmer viaduct. It is not known to which branch of the family Morgan James belonged, but as Thomas Leyshon has pointed out the *Established 1750* on the company's old official correspondence is a clear indication of a connection. There was no woollen factory at Maesycwmmer until 1841; 1750 was the date when old Evan James's father established his factory in Caerphilly.

Many of the brothers wrote poetry and three – John, Daniel and James - emigrated to the United States.

In 1832, at the age of 23, Evan James, the son, married Elizabeth Jones of Eglwysilan. The warmth of a letter from an older brother, Lewis James, to Evan and his wife suggests that she was well respected by the James family. We know little more than that about her, except that she was a devout member of Carmel Welsh Baptist Chapel, that they had seven children – and that she

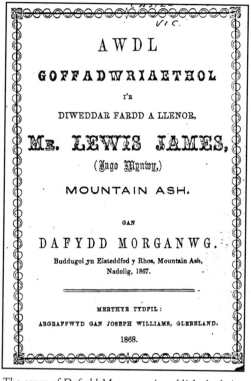

AWDL

GOFFADWRIAETHOL

I'R

DIWEDDAR FARDD A LLENOR,

MR. LEWIS JAMES,

(Iago Mynwy,)

MOUNTAIN ASH.

GAN

DAFYDD MORGANWG.

Buddugol yn Eisteddfod y Rhos, Mountain Ash,
Nadolig, 1867.

MERTHYR TYDFIL :

ARGRAFFWYD GAN JOSEPH WILLIAMS, GLEBELAND.

1868.

The cover of Dafydd Morganwg's published ode in memory of Lewis, brother of Evan James

was a woman of formidable proportions! Evan writes Argoed along with his name under his early poems, which suggests that he was living there before he married. In the years 1833-35 he writes Aberbargoed under the poems and it was there, at the Old Inn, that he was living when his first son James (Iago ab Ieuan) was baptized in St Catwg's Church, Gelligaer, in 1833, and Daniel was baptized in 1835. I assume that Daniel died in infancy as I found no subsequent reference to him. Evan's occupation is described as weaver. In 1836, Evan and his family moved to the Ancient Druid Inn, Argoed, where the old family had lived when Evan was a child, and possibly for a time before he married. As Evan returned there, certainly after his marriage, it appears likely that the family had retained possession of the inn and the surrounding buildings – described as an inn, factory and cottages.

In the above mentioned letter to Evan and Blodwen James, the relatives in Washington, the Rev Gwilym Thomas described one of the family's customs during this period: "For many years Yr Hen Dafarn (The Old Inn) was the chief centre of the James's family. All the brothers kept in close touch with their sister, a grand annual feast was held (every Easter) at Yr Hen Dafarn known as Pasti'r Bont. This feast lasted for a week. The young people of the district came there night after night to have a good meal, and to sing and dance to the harp. Your grandfather (Evan James, writer of the anthem) attended the feast regularly."

Yr Hen Dafarn was the inn at Pontaberbargoed, situated at the confluence of Nant Bargoed and the Rhymni, although I have been told that the original inn was a little further upstream. Its present name is Gold Mine! Dr Emrys Thomas (son of the Rev Gwilym Thomas) explains that Mary, Evan's only sister to survive infancy, kept the inn. She had married Thomas Lewis, the son of the inn. It was only about half a mile from the woollen factory kept by Edward and Mary James, and the inn became a centre for the James family – the only daughter keeping the brothers in touch with one another. With everyone coming together every Easter to sing, write poetry, dance to the harp, feast and drink home-brewed beer. Calfaria Congregational Chapel, Aberbargoed, incidentally, was founded in a room in *Yr Hen Dafarn* in 1870. When the railway came the station was named Bargoed and the village name of Pontaberbargoed eventually became Bargoed, too. Aberbargoed is the name of the part of Bargoed on the eastern side of the river Rhymni, which was formerly in Monmouthshire.

Pontaberbargoed lle hynod y byd,
Pum tŷ tafarn sydd yno i gyd,
Dwy siop ragorol a gof a thŷ crydd,
Melin a phandy, tri jac a thri swydd.

(Pontaberbargoed, best place in the world,
Just five inns there are in total,
Two splendid shops, a smith and a cobbler,
A mill and a fulling-mill, three (weaving) jacks
and three offices (?).)

That is how Lewis James, one of Evan's older brothers, described the village of Aberbargoed at that time. Lewis and Evan were obviously very close to each other in their interests, opinions and beliefs, and he is worthy of a mention in the story of the Jameses. Dafydd Morganwg (David Watkin Jones, 1832-1905), poet and historian, won the prize for an elegy to the memory of Lewis James – or Iago Mynwy as he is referred to – at the Christmas 1867 Rhos Eisteddfod, Mountain Ash. The ode was published as a pamphlet the following year. It is a sign of Lewis's status that poets were invited to write an ode in his memory and that the poet Dafydd Morganwg, author of *Hanes Morganwg* (History of Glamorgan) and *Yr Ysgol Farddol* (The Bardic School), saw fit to submit a poem. The pamphlet is useful, not only for the ode, written in the traditional metres, but because it contains a biography of Lewis James. It is noted that he was born in Caerphilly in August 1798. He is described as having had a good elementary education of which he made good use. When the family moved from Caerphilly he learnt the craft of shoemaker. At the age of 22 he married Catherine Jones of Llanhilleth, and after a while settled in Argoed. About the same time a *Cymreigyddion* (Literary) Society was established in the home of his brother David James (Dewi ab

Iago), The Factory, Argoed. Lewis built an inn in Cwm Rhydderch, Ebbw Vale, which was named The Boot – presumably because he continued to follow his craft as a cobbler and shoemaker in the same place, just as Evan at times was both a publican and a weaver.

In 1836, about the time Lewis moved to Ebbw Vale, the Wrexham Union of the True Order of Ivorites (*Undeb Gwerfyl Gwrexham o Urdd y Gwir Iforiaid*), was established. This was a mainly working class charitable organisation (see also p. 106 in which all activities were conducted in the Welsh language. Lewis joined the Order, and a branch named after Dafydd ap Gwilym – the 14th century romantic poet – was formed in his house. The Ivorites played an influential part in Evan James's life, too. In 1840, there was a split in the Order between the Dewi Sant union in Carmarthen and the Wrexham branch and Lewis was an eloquent supporter of the Wrexham group. He moved from Ebbw Vale to Rhondda or Pontypridd and from there went to keep The New Inn in Mountain Ash. He was closely involved in local affairs and was an effective, generous and respected Parish Guardian within the Merthyr and Pontypridd Union. As well as his work with the Ivorites he was also an active member of the Oddfellows. He was very supportive of Welsh literature and often presided at Eisteddfodau and Literary Gartherings. "Had he a motto," the biography says, "it would have been 'My language, my country, my nation'."

In 1847 there came an important change to the life of Evan James when he and his family moved to Pontypridd. For that he – and all of us – should be thankful to Lewis. Had the family not moved to Pontypridd, who knows, maybe Wales would still be without a national anthem. Evan and Elizabeth received a letter from Lewis, from *Pontybridd*, dated September 20, 1847, written in a slightly archaic, elegant

Welsh. The following translation is from Thomas T. Leyshon's book *Bridges to Harps to Millionaires.*

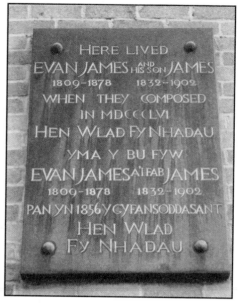

Dear Brother and Sister, I hope you are still in good health as we are. The purpose of this letter is to let you know that the Factory held by Thos Austin is to be rented and its owner wishes me to offer it to you. There are others who are keen on having it. The price is forty pounds a year. A house will be part of it, and it will

The plaque on the wall of the Pontypridd building where once stood Evan James's factory

be spacious enough. There is 1 Scribbler, 1 Carder, 1 Tucker, 2 Weaving Jacks, 1 Skainer, 2 Colouring Furnaces, and a Washing Boiler. T. Austin will recommend you to all his customers, and he will also let you know where he purchased for the purpose of the factory. His reason for selling is that he was offered a large sum for it, nine hundred pounds, and that because of his small family there was no need for him to labour much more. In my opinion you will not receive a better proposition than this if you are contemplating selling the "Druid" and acquiring a Factory.

I am not trying to persuade you to do this for my own sake, nor for the sake of anyone else, but solely for your sake, dear Brother and Sister and your growing family, because I cannot see that your present place is as good as this one for bringing up the dear ones under your care. Philip Holland the weaver was paying thirteen pounds a quarter to T. Austin for spinning, without mentioning the market which is adjacent, and the country work, as well as the opportunity to send to the fulling mill every market day free of expense. Consider also that this is the best time for selling the "Druid". This is what I consider my duty for your sake.

Lewis James

I would like you to send your reply as soon as you can.

Among other papers and documents appertaining to Evan James in the National Library in Aberystwyth there is a copy of a draft contract made between Ebenezer Williams, *brewer*, and Evan James, *publican and woollen-manufacturer*, showing that Evan took at a rent of £45 a year, for a period of 14 years beginning on November 1, 1847, *the Woollen Manufactory and residence situated in Mill Street in Newbridge aforesaid together with the stock and plant and other implements of the trade.* Note that Lewis James writes *Pontybridd* but Newbridge is the name on the contract. There has been some debate as to which is the original name. It is likely that both were used at one time, Pontypridd by Welsh speakers, Newbridge by English speakers. Both names are certainly very old.

The date 1735 on the *Newbridge Arms* in Trallwm, Pontypridd, suggests that the name Newbridge is older than William Edwards's celebrated single-span bridge across the Taff, which he completed in 1756. There was a wooden bridge across the Taff a little further stream from which the name of the *Newbridge Arms* probably came. But the name Pont-y-tŷ-pridd is older that 1735. Around 1700 Edward Llwyd sent a questionnaire to the clerks of all the parish councils in Wales. One of his questions was about bridges within their parishes. He received a reply from the clerk of Aberdare Parish Council

– which included Llanwynno – which mentioned a bridge on the periphery of the parish with the name Pont-y-tŷ-pridd. He also received a reply from the clerk of Llantwit Faerdre Parish Council, also referring to a bridge of the same name on the edge of the parish. As the river Rhondda would have been the boundary between the two parishes, it seems almost certain that Pont-y-tŷ-pridd was a bridge across that river somewhere near its confluence with the Taff. But soon after it had been built the name Pont-y-tŷ-pridd must have been adopted for William Edwards's bridge. Edward Ifan (1716-1798), the poet from Ton Coch, Aberdare, wrote a series of *englynion* to Pont-y-tŷ-pridd, and although I have been unable to date them, there is no doubt that he was writing about William Edwards's bridge.

Of course, the Brown Lenox factory established in 1818 was known as the **Newbridge** *Chain and Anchor Works*. *Newbridge* was the name given to the train station opened in 1840, and *Newbridge* is the name on the maps of the time. But those responsible for such decisions would have been English. The decision to adopt *Pontypridd* as the town's official and only name was taken by the Pontypridd Postmaster, Charles Bassett, who had had enough of letters going astray among all the towns with the name *Newbridge*. He made his decision in 1856, the year *Hen Wlad Fy Nhadau* was composed, and one hundred years after William Edwards completed his bridge, the bridge which had become known as *Pont-y-tŷ-pridd* and which was attracting artists and writers to the area long before the town was established. But enough of that, Evan James and his family in 1847 came to a little town in a ferment of cultural activity. The full blast of the industrial revolution had yet to hit Pontypridd.

Pontypridd in the mid-19th century

Evan James's name was known before he came to live in the town with which his name indelibly linked. Among the Evan James manuscripts in the National Library there are two poems welcoming him to the town. A poet calling himself Eos y Dyffryn begins:

> *Hawddamor fad ddedwyddawl ddydd*
> *Y deuaist Ieuan, fywlon fardd,*
> *Ab Iago i drigo'm Mhontypridd –*
> *Am hyn o'i mewn llawenydd dardd.*

> (All hail fine and blissful day
> Thou comest Ieuan, lively bard,
> Ab Iago, to live in Pontypridd –
> For this within me joy eternal springs.)

Pontypridd, compared to neighbouring Merthyr Tydfil and Aberdare, is a comparatively new town. When William Edwards completed his bridge in 1756 this was green, wooded country with Taff's waters flowing clear in its rocky bed. It was the Brown Lenox chainworks founded in 1818 alongside the Cardiff-Merthyr canal, that gave Pontypridd its early impetus. Treforest, with its first ironworks founded in 1803 and where Francis Crawshay later came to oversee his father's tin and ironworks, grew earlier and more quickly. The arrival of the Cardiff-Merthyr railway and the opening of Pontypridd's train station in 1840 was the next important milestone in the town's development. As more and more deep coalmines were sunk in the Rhondda Valleys and around Pontypridd, the town grew with frightening speed from 1880

William Edwards's bridge was completed in 1756, a hundred years before the anthem was composed

onwards swamped by a wave of English immigrants the like of which no other town in industrial South Wales had experienced. By the end of the century 300 trains a day stopped in Pontypridd's smoky and noisy station. By 1901 the town's population had doubled.

A high percentage of Welsh-speakers from the countryside had flocked to the ironworks of Merthyr and Dowlais in 1758, and to the Garn Furnace in the Cynon Valley in 1762 followed by other small furnaces and later to the giant ironworks of Llwydcoed (1799) and Abernant (1800). In the Rhondda Valleys other men were digging for coal. By the time Pontypridd was really expanding rural Wales had been bled dry of men and women who wanted – or needed – to leave their farms. The immigration from England and Ireland was on a huge scale – particularly to Treforest with its Irish community, reflected in its large Catholic Church.

An old painting of the Brunel railway bridge across the Rhondda. Evan James's factory was one of the buildings backing on to the river.

Pontypridd, by the beginning of the 20th century, was the most Anglicised of all the Glamorgan towns.

But to return to an earlier era, Thomas Evans in *The History of Miskin Higher* shows that the image of Pontypridd as a village of a few scattered houses, a smithy, inn, shop and a mill is not accurate either. The Llanwynno Parish Rate Book for 1842 lists 35 houses and shops in Market Street, 64 in Taff Street, 17 in Bridge Street, 13 in Crossbrook Street and 55 in Mill Street as well as a number of inns, blacksmiths, carpenters and a wheelwright, one abattoir and a number of farms. This was two years after the railway came in 1840. In *The Rise and Progress of Nonconformity in Pontypridd and District* the Rev Benjamin Davies appears to be making a reasonable estimate that the population of that part of Pontypridd that was in the parish of Hafod Ddriniog, including children, could not have exceeded 3,400 in 1861. By including figures from the parts of the town that were in the parishes of Llantrisant, Llantwit Faerdre and Eglwysilan the population of the town would not have been more than 4,000, according to Davies. It is later that Pontypridd grew into a kind of frontier town, between the old Welsh-speaking villages and farms and the English newcomers. Some of those villages retained their Welshness for another hundred years. I recall going to the shop in Pentyrch in the 1970s and finding everyone, including the shopkeeper speaking Welsh – they were not incomers, but the indigenous community, speaking the lovely dialect of Glamorgan and Gwent. I remember the landlady of the Brynffynnon Arms in Llanwynno speaking Welsh and many – some still alive – descendents of the original population of Llantwit Faerdre who have retained the language. Cilfynydd and Ynysybwl retained their Welsh-speaking enclaves almost to this day. When Evan James brought his family to Pontypridd in the middle of the 19th century, these communities – and most of Pontypridd – were completely Welsh in language.

Speaking the same language was a class of craftsmen, shopkeepers and solicitors who brought with them their culture and eccentric vivacity – many were contemporaries of Evan James, others had arrived earlier and some came later. They brought with them lively minds and impressive literary activity. Huw Walters describes in *Merthyr a Thaf* how the Eisteddfod and the literary groups became important institutions in the industrial towns and villages. These newcomers refreshed the literary activities and aspirations in the Glamorgan of the *triban* – a four line poetic form once exclusive to these parts – the harp and the *noson lawen* – a spontaneous concert where anyone could, and often expected, to participate. They also provided a major boost to the Eisteddfodau – large and small. The Eisteddfodau had been relatively small events, dominated by poets. Now their musical content was exanding and with choirs came bigger crowds. The growth of a weekly and periodical press in Merthyr, Aberdare and Pontypridd gave an opportunity for these poets to see their works in print.

Among the incomers were people like Thomas Williams (Gwilym Morganwg), a miller's son from the Parish of Landdety, Breconshire, who came to Pontypridd around 1807 and kept the New Inn until his death in 1835. The extraordinary stonemason, druid, poet, forger, romantic mythmaker and genius Edward Williams (Iolo Morganwg, 1747-1826) had cast his spell over these characters. Iolo, himself, had been intrigued by the Rocking Stone on Coedpenmaen Common above Pontypridd. These two stones – the geological term is erratics – were carried by an ice age and left, one balanced on top of the other, when the ice retreated. By jumping energetically on the top stone it is still possible to make it rock a little. *"Most of us are of the opinion that in former times it was a Druidic Gorsedd* (meeting place, literally

The Rocking Stone

throne)," wrote Gwilym Morganwg – doubtless echoing the opinions of Iolo – in a letter published in *Seren Gomer*, February 8, 1815. Iolo held two meetings of his *Gorsedd* at the Rocking Stone in 1814, one in August and the other on December 21, and another there in 1817.

A year later, in 1818, Iolo organised a *Gorsedd* in the grounds of the Ivy Bush in Carmarthen, coinciding with the Carmarthen Eisteddfod and bringing the two institutions together for the first time. They have remained linked together ever since. It was at the Carmarthen Eisteddfod that Gwilym Morganwg came to national prominence as Bearer of the Sword. But it was in Pontypridd, in the New Inn, that he held court. This was his power base, where the poets gathered and organised their Eisteddfodau from time to time. He played a key role at the beginning of the 1830s in founding *Cymdeithas Cymreigyddion y Maen Chwŷf* (The Rocking Stone Literary Society, Maen Chwŷf translates literally as Moving Stone). They organised their own Eisteddfodau, attracting the likes of Aneurin Jones (Aneurin Sion or Aneurin Fardd) after whom it is said Aneurin Bevan was named. Whether they were actually related is not clear, but David Bevan, Aneurin Bevan's father, was a friend of Aneurin Fardd, a Welsh speaker and Eisteddfod competitor. Among other enthusiastic competitors at these Eisteddfodau were Gwilym Llanwynno (Thomas Evans) and Meudwy Glan Elái (Evan Richards).

The remarkable Dr William Price, brilliant surgeon, druid and Chartist, born in Tynycoedcae, near Machen, Monmouthshire, was another who had been drawn to Pontypridd. He is best remembered for attempting to burn his dead baby, named Jesus Christ, in Llantrisant, and for the ensuing furore and court case as a result of which cremation became legal. But he deserves to be remembered, just as much, for his pioneering work providing a health service for ironworkers and coalminers in Treforest and Pontypridd. It was a health service to which the workers themselves contributed when they were healthy and in work and received free treatment from Price when they fell ill. It was a scheme adopted by The Tredegar Medical Assistance Society, which in turn inspired Aneurin Bevan's National Health Service. Price was also infatuated by druidism, although there is no record that he was ever invested as a member of any *Gorsedd*. He became incensed when Evan Davies (Ieuan Myfyr, and who later gave himself the grander bardic name of Myfyr Morganwg) assumed the title of Archdruid in 1849, since Price had given himself the title some time earlier. This caused some tension between the two, which was to be repeated a second time after the death of Myfyr and Owen Morgan (Morien) took up the mantle. As a result William Price, continued until the end of his life to conduct his own ceremonies at the Rocking Stone. It has been suggested that there were some psychological reasons for the eccentric behaviour of these people – a reaction to the encroaching Anglicisation and seeing the Welsh language and culture increasingly under siege. Others may come to different conclusions. But we would do well to remember that Iolo Morganwg's vision for his *Gorsedd* probably owed as much to the early ideals of the French Revolution as to any extant information about Druidism which can be gleaned from the writings of the Romans.

Ieuan Myfyr (Edward Davies) was a clock-maker and repairer. His notebooks in Cardiff Central Library and the grandfather clock in Pontypridd Museum are testimony to his craftsmanship. But he had other, consuming, interests. He had been invested into the bardic circle by Taliesin ab Iolo (Taliesin Williams, son of Iolo Morganwg) in a *Gorsedd* held at the Rocking Stone in 1834 and by Cawrdaf (William Ellis Jones,

1795-1848) at Cowbridge in 1839. He was a sufficiently vociferous critic of the temperance movement to incur the wrath of the Rev John Jones (Jones Llangollen) and the two engaged in a public debate on the subject in Llantrisant in November 1842. Myfyr, who was no drunkard and even preached from the pulpits of the local chapels, argued for moderation – not total abstinence. He came to Pontypridd in 1846 to set up a shop and a workshop in Mill Street, where Evan James was to settle a year later. Aneurin Fardd was awarded a prize for a poem welcoming Myfyr to the town at Eisteddfod y Maen Chwŷf held on August 10, 1846. Myfyr, following in the wake of the neo-druidism of Iolo Morganwg and Taliesin ab Iolo, also took a profound interest in Hinduism as well as Druidism and by adding dollops of Christianity came up with a rich and strange theological mix.

After the death of Taliesin ab Iolo and Carnhuanawc (Rev Thomas Price) the Druids and the leading lights of the

The New Inn, Mountain Ash, the pub kept by Lewis, brother of Evan James

Eisteddfod in Glamorgan and Gwent lost their cultural leaders and it was Myfyr who leapt into the breach. In years to come, he would insist that the Glamorgan *Gorsedd* had greater authority than those of the regional Eisteddfodau, even than the National Eisteddfod, because of its direct link to Iolo Morganwg, creator of modern druidism, the Gorsedd and its ceremonies. In 1849 Myfyr and his friends cleared the site around the Rocking Stone, held meetings at the Summer and Winter Solstices and the Spring and Autumn Equinoxes, erected two circles of standing stones around it and then erected a narrow avenue of stones in the form of a serpent leading to the serpent's "head" with eyes and three stones in the form of the *Gorsedd* mystical mark / | \ . Then he announced that the *Gorsedd* of Glamorgan was invested with authority over all the *Gorseddau* of the Isle of Britain and that a meeting of poets and druids would be held on the site the following year. This was duly done on the Summer Solstice of 1850 and Ieuan Myfyr officiated at the first gathering of his *Gorsedd. The licensed bards, among them Ieuan Myfyr who carried the sword, Gwilym Ilid (William Jones), Nathan Dyfed (Jonathan Reynolds), Dewi Haran (David Evans) and Ioan Emlyn (Rev John Emlyn Jones) along with other honourable persons ... ovates and other responsible literati walked in a splendid bannered procession from the New Inn to the Rocking Stone.* The *Gorsedd* ceremony began in *accordance with custom* after which Myfyr offered a Prayer – the first time for this to be done at a meeting of any *Gorsedd,* according to the former Archdruid and *Gorsedd* historian, Geraint Bowen. Gwyddonwyson (Rev David Rhys Stephens) a Baptist Minister in Abercarn was approved to the Druidic Order, and five were invested to the Order of Bards, among them Evan James (Ieuan ab Iago) and Thomas Essile Davies (Dewi Wyn o Essyllt). Dewi, originally from Dinas Powis, was another of that class of shopkeepers and

The Llanover Arms, a favourite pub of the Pontypridd poets. At one time it may have been kept by Thomas, one of Evan James's younger brothers.

merchants who came to Pontypridd to take advantage of its growing importance as a market town for the industrialised Rhondda and surrounding valleys and villages. It was, however, sometime after 1850 before he came to live in the town. At various times he had been, among other occupations, a miller and a shopkeeper. He is best remembered as a prolific poet – some of his odes in traditional metres ran to a thousand lines – who was quite successful as a competitor at Eisteddfodau. He dropped dead while calling for a quick pint in the Hewitt Arms, Penycoedcae, on his way home to Pontypridd on the night of January 30, 1891.

Pontypridd in those days was, in the words of Harri Webb, "a centre of the rich delicious nonsense of Druidism, as elaborated by the credulous followers of Iolo Morganwg, lesser men with all the weaknesses and none of the greatness of Iolo". Harri goes on to insist that Evan "avoids every pitfall

90

... he has nothing to say about Druids". Not so. Evan was at the Rocking Stone on the Summer Solstice of 1850 being invested by Ieuan Myfyr into the Order of Bards, and his son James was admitted into the Order of Ovates, according to Dilwyn Miles, another *Gorsedd* and Eisteddfod historian. Not only that, on the Autumn Equinox he was addressing the assembled druids and poets with an ode in the old metres. Among his considerable body of unpublished works can be found poems in praise of Druids and Druidism.

While Iolo Morganwg, Taliesin ab Iolo, Ieuan Myfyr – who in 1853 gave himself the bardic name Myfyr Morganwg - and the Druids were holding their ceremonies at the Rocking Stone there were other poets meeting informally, in parallel with the *Gorsedd*, in the town. Who knows which came first, Iolo and his *Gorsedd* or the lively and witty literary circle that became known as *Clic y Bont* (The clique of the Bont). For decades, Pontypridd had been a centre for poets from the Taff Vale, Eglwysilan, Llanfabon, Cilfynydd, Llantrisant and Rhondda. Doubtless, these poets found the pomp of the Rocking Stone *Gorsedd* attractive and reckoned it added to their honour and dignity. "They were drawn together by the herding instinct of poets," wrote the Rev John Dyfnallt Owen. *Clic y Bont* was an informal muse and music club. I have already mentioned the poets who met in the New Inn and the Eisteddfodau held there in the time of Gwilym Morganwg. In an Eisteddfod in The Fairoak, one of the inns of Trehafod, the village between Pontypridd and Porth, Ioan Emlyn won a few shillings for his poem *Bedd y Dyn Tylawd* (The Pauper's Grave), a poem that became well known and was included later in W. J. Gruffydd's standard anthology, *Y Flodeugerdd Gymraeg*.

As the population – and the chapels – multiplied the literary meetings and the Eisteddfodau became more and more a part of the chapel activities. The preachers and ministers grabbed the reins as poets and adjudicators, taking over from the old generous benefactors of the public houses. In the words of John Dyfnallt Owen, "The Eisteddfod went into the chapel: the harp remained in the pub, and this was a disaster for the ready wit of the poets, the folk songs and poems." But the humorous members of *Clic y Bont* never lost their wit or sense of mischief. Their haunts were *The New Inn* and the *Llanover Arms*. A harp, I have been told, would be brought out and played in the *Llanover Arms* on Friday nights as recently as the 1930s. Myfyr Morganwg, Dewi Wyn o Essyllt, Dewi Haran and ap Myfyr (John Davies, son of Myfyr) were some of the leading members in the 1850s and 1860s and we can assume that Evan James took some part in their activities. In the latter period some of the better-known members included Dewi Davies (Dewi Alaw), Thomas Williams (Brynfab) and Coslett Coslett (Carnelian). Dewi Alaw, although he lived most of his life in poverty scraping a living as a peddler, was a man of some genius, a fine poet in the traditional metres and an equally accomplished musician.

Not everyone approved of the *Clic*. It was probably William Henry Dyer (Mabonwyson) who first called them a clique. Mabonwyson had been to college in preparation for the ministry – on the whole, the *Clic* did not approve of those who had spent too much time in formal education. He took his revenge, in the lovely dialect of Glamorgan, when he gave his own colourful description of some of its members, a description in which, sadly, a lot gets lost in translation:

Dewi Wyn o Essyllt keeping a tiny shop in Llanfana, all he sells is soap and treacle, with his entire shop in the window. Dewi Haran, a bit of a dealer and auctioneer, whose job is telling lies, and he'd sell his mother for a ha'penny. Dewi Alaw peddling about the Bont with an old horse and cart the Clic had bought for him, and the horse so thin you could play a tune on his ribs. Carnelian, a bit of a collier working a level on the side of Graigwen, and not cutting enough coal to keep a barber's fire alight; and Brynfab with a tiny farm on the side of Eglwysilan Mountain that I could cover with my hat."

Brynfab's farm was Hendre Prysor, above Rhydfelen, from where came the dry stone Glamorgan pigsty which can be seen at the Museum of Welsh Life at St Fagan's. It appears that Mabonwyson had a rather grand hat, large enough to serve as an umbrella as well, and an inspiration to the poets:

> *Yn ei het mae'i awen o – a gwesgir*
> *O dan gysgod honno*
> *Bethau od, mae'n gwb a tho,*
> *Barilau, ac ymbarelo.*

> (In his hat is his muse – and squeezed
>   Beneath its shadow
> Are strange things, it's a coop and roof,
> A barrel and umbrella.)

Mabonwyson suffered merciless leg pulling from the *Clic*. He often spoke of his intentions to go and visit his cousins in America, and in 1875 the *Clic* held an Eisteddfod in his honour in the Malster's Arms, Pontypridd. The subjects of all the literary competitions were to do with Mabonwyson: A Nation Laments his Departure, The Sea-voyage, The Delight of the Americans at his Arrival in their Midst, even an elegy in his memory in the event that he might drown during the journey! As Mabonwyson had yet to embark on his journey he was invited to adjudicate the literary entries – an invitation he accepted. The generosity of the *Clic* knew no bounds. Mabonwyson was even offered the proceeds of the event – perhaps in hope that this would hurry him on his way – but as it was a miserable sum Mabonwyson – in a huff – refused it. It was decided to spend the money on a dinner and according to an amusing report in *Y Gwladgarwr*, if Mabonwyson's pocket was at a loss, at least his stomach was well pleased. As far as we know Mabonwyson never went to America.

At the end of the 19th century Dewi Alaw could list 139 poets who had lived in and around Pontypridd since 1850. They were categorised as follows: Rhymesters; writers of the traditional Glamorgan *Triban*; others who could be relied on to produce something adequate with which to address a gathering of, for example, The Ivorites; and those blessed by the *true muse*.

"Clic y Bont was a bird's nest," wrote Dyfnallt. "Some were motley enough. Their voices were sometimes a little rough. In behaviour, bohemians; in belief, pagans in the aesthetic sense, but proud to be in the succession of the old poets, fostering a taste for a well-turned line or couplet, and feeding the immortal passion of the ancient Welsh for a tale and a song, a tune on the harp and good company among congenial souls."

They belonged to the romantic tradition. They regretted the coming of industrialisation and the destruction of an old rural way of life. Glanffrwd (William Thomas, 1843–1890) in his classic little history of *The Parish of Llanwynno* wrote of his dismay and revulsion at the effects of the industrial revolution:

"O! My dear Llanwynno, you too at last have sunk beneath the feet of the enemy. The sanctity of your beautiful fields have been trampled, your melodious birds driven away, the fiery stallions neighed, and screams like a thousand pigs have been heard in your lovely glades! So fair, so peaceful, so pure, so silent, so dear were you before the adventurers came to burrow your breast! And now, you are like – well, like all places where coal is to be found."

Such sentiments were echoed by many of the *Clic* – not

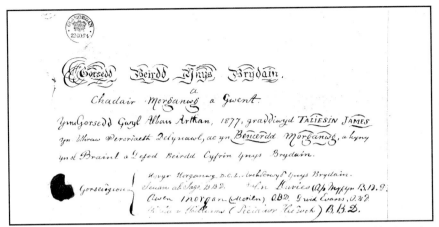

Taliesin James's certificate of membership of the Rocking Stone Gorsedd, signed by Myfyr Morganwg, Evan James and Morien

least by the keen critic and witty and talented poet Brynfab. His semi-autobiographical novel *Pan Oedd Rhondda'n Bur* (When Rhondda was Pure), is a romantic picture of a green and remote, rural, Welsh-speaking, valley.

A similarly romantic view of the old rural way of life runs through much of Evan James's poetry. But his attitude towards the new industrialisation was not as negative as that of the *Clic*. Industry brought people, people brought business, and Evan was a business man.

The festivals of the Glamorgan Druids, presided over by Myfyr Morganwg, at the Rocking Stone had begun in earnest in 1850. Then, in 1851, a young man named Henry Oliver was ordained minister of Sardis, the Welsh Congregational Chapel in Pontypridd. He was one of the first two Welsh graduates of London University, clever, talented, fervent Non-conformist, eloquent preacher and reformer. He found the goings-on at the common intolerable and set about exposing the superstition. Myfyr was furious issuing challenges to the Reverend. Oliver responded, and Myfyr threatened to bring the wrath of the gods down on his head.

Oliver challenged the gods to do their worst. According to Dyfnallt Owen: "The sun dimmed on the Common; the pulpit won and the Rocking Stone lost; Druidism began to lose its charm for the poets and as in ancient Greece, the poets said farewell to the old gods."

Others suggest it was not quite so clear-cut or straightforward. To the dismay of the Non-conformist ministers of Taff and Rhondda, Myfyr Morganwg and his followers continued to conduct their ceremonies at the Rocking Stone for almost another 30 years. B. D. Johns (Periander) in his *Early History of the Rhondda Valley: Baptist Centenary, Pontypridd 1810-1910* went so far as to state that a wave of druidism had swept through the town between 1866 and 1876 resulting in a serious decline in chapel membership. And Thomas Evans wrote in *The History of Miskin Higher:* "In 1859, the year of the great revival, the membership at Carmel under the Rev Edward Roberts, D.D. was 329 and in 1860 it rose to 394. The following year, a wave of modern Druidism swept through Pontypridd, depriving the churches of many members. It took many years to repair the loss." D. M. Williams wrote a letter in the July 2, 1875, edition of *Y Gwladarwr* (*An Address to the Ministers of Pontypridd and District*), calling for a meeting of the town's ministers to discuss what was to be done with those who "were sowing the seeds of atheism, and planting anti-Biblical principles in the minds of the weak and the young." And the Rev R. G. Hughes, Minister of Capel Rhondda, Hopkinstown, was writing in *Llawlyfr Cyfarfod Blynyddol Undeb Bedyddwyr Cymru a Mynwy* (Handbook of the Annual Meeting of the Baptist Union of Wales and Monmouthshire), held in Tabernacl, Pontypridd, September 9-12, 1935, "That the Druids had held great influence in the area; but their influence vanished years ago".

Myfyr Morganwg died in 1888. His successor was

Owen Morgan (Morien), a talented journalist with the *Western Mail* and the author of *History of Pontypridd and District* and various weird and wonderful volumes, in Welsh and English, on the subject of Druidism. According to Dyfnallt, Morien's relationship with *Clic y Bont* was conducted at arm's length. The poets, among them *Clic y Bont*, were turning away from Druidism, and for Morien that was unforgivable. Morien had been invested a member of the Druidic Order of the Gorsedd of the National Eisteddfod in 1888 with the bardic name of *Gwyddon Tir Iarll* (Wizard of Tir Iarll), in the vain hope, suggests Huw Walters, that he might relinquish the title of Archdruid of the Rocking Stone Gorsedd! Morien continued to preside over his Gorsedd in Pontypridd. He was given a prominent part in the ceremonies of the National Eisteddfod Gorsedd when it came to Pontypridd in 1893.

Pontypridd's 120-year Druidic tradition ended with the death of Morien in 1921. Years that had seen much amusing – and sometimes vitriolic – debate in the press. Although it should be said that the reports of the *Gorsedd* activities in the English language local press were at best sympathetic, at worst mild bemusement. The Welsh language press was more critical. Morien, in a later period, often felt the need to respond and never flinched from taking up the cudgels and debate the history and antiquity of the Gorsedd with the formidable John Morris-Jones in Welsh language journals. Whatever we might think of Morien, today, he was emphatic and sincere in his beliefs and at a time when the National Eisteddfod was becoming ever more Anglicised the Gorsedd, whether of the National Eisteddfod or of the Pontypridd Rocking Stone, never deviated in its absolute support of the Welsh language.

There is no doubt that Evan James took an active part in these ceremonies. Three months after he was invested a member of Myfyr Morganwg's Gorsedd in 1850 he was addressing the assembled poets and druids with an ode in traditional metres. *The Cambrian* newspaper describes James James playing his harp at the Rocking Stone during the 1860 Eisteddfod, held on June 21. Evan's love of the Welsh language, the central theme of *Hen Wlad Fy Nhadau*, is in tune with the main principles and objectives of the *Gorseddau*. He wrote – unpublished – poems in defence and in praise of Druids and Druidism, poems that refer quite directly to press criticism. It is interesting to recall that Mrs Elizabeth James was a devout member of Carmel Baptist Chapel, and when Carmel changed from a Welsh to an English chapel, did she go with many of the other Welsh-speaking members, to Tabernacl, the chapel by William Edwards's bridge now the Pontypridd Museum? Tabernacl's minister was the Rev Edward Roberts, D.D., who fiercely condemned the Druids from the pulpit. We can only wonder whether Mrs James was present, listening to these savage denunciations while her husband and eldest son at the same time were with Myfyr Morganwg and the Druids on the Common.

There must have been some conflict within the ministerial fraternity itself. Some ministers were more than happy to associate with the Druids; Ioan Emlyn (Rev John Emlyn Jones), the brilliant poet, preacher and academic, was one of the "licensed" poets who was in the procession of *"honourable persons ...ovates and other responsible literati"* who walked from The New Inn to the Rocking Stone in 1850. Two years later he was invited to be Minister of Capel Rhondda, Hopkinstown!

Evan James was more than happy to insert after his name the letters B.B.D. (*Bardd Braint a Defod* – Bard by Privilege and Rite), the bardic degree that Iolo Morganwg had devised for himself. When Taliesin James (1857-1938), son of James James, was invested a member of *Gorsedd Beirdd Ynys*

Prydain a Chadair Morganwg a Gwent (Gorsedd of the Bards of the Isle of Britain and the Chair of Glamorgan and Gwent) on the Winter Solstice of 1877, Evan, in the year before his death was one of the three signatories of Taliesin's certificate. Myfyr and Morien were the other two, and all three signed their names, with the letters B.B.D. after their names. Taliesin went on to the Royal Academy of Music in London where he was a student of the harpist John Thomas (Pencerdd Gwalia). Taliesin was later invested a member of the *Gorsedd* of the National Eisteddfod with the bardic name Pencerdd Morgannwg. After a period of time as landlord of *The Swan* in Aberaman he was invited to become the harp tutor at University College, Cardiff. His harp, made by the French brothers Sebastian and Pierre Erard, was eventually given to Ysgol Uwchradd Gymraeg Rhydfelen, Pontypridd, the first Welsh medium secondary school in South Wales. After a time it was decided that the harp was too valuable and fragile for daily use by school pupils and is now in the care of Pontypridd Museum where it is still played on special occasions.

Evan James, man and poet

Evan James appears to have been a well-respected employer in the town of Pontypridd – in spite of occasional critical comments about strikes in the margins of his account books. Although strikes for higher wages and better working conditions were becoming increasingly common there is no evidence that there was any conflict between him and his workers. Of course, he was hardly a major employer of workers. And although a regular frequenter of the gatherings at the Rocking Stone a picture emerges of a likeable person, tending to stay in the background and working hard to make a success of his business – one that grew to become quite prosperous.

Politically, the ideas and influences of Tom Paine can be seen in Evan James. Religiously, too, there seems to be in the deism of Paine much that Evan would have found acceptable. In England, Paine is viewed as an extreme revolutionary. In reality he was – if that is not too much of a contradiction in terms – a moderate revolutionary. *"Universal peace, civilization and commerce"* were, in his view, the answer to the world's ills. War and high taxes were the root of all evil and private enterprise was *"the most effectual process ... of improving the condition of man"*. His book *The Age of Reason* in 1794, as pointed out by Eric Hobsbawm, *"became the first book to say flatly, in language comprehensible to the common people, that the Bible was not the word of God."* Paine was of the class to whom he was writing – a self-made, self-educated, self-reliant man who had successively, and reasonably successfully dabbled in a variety of occupations. He opposed privilege, which he saw as an obstacle to "freedom". He belonged to a class of skilled artisans, small shopkeepers and farmers who were confident enough to believe that the future lay in their hands. Poverty was a collective fact, a problem to be solved, not one from which to escape. Paine had an uncomplicated vision, an *obvious* truth – that what the priests say about the Bible, or the rich about society, is wrong. We can assume that Evan James was familiar with Paine's *Age of Reason* and *Rights of Man*, he seems to be quite in tune with Paine's thinking.

Evan James appears to have been a rather reserved person. Although he wrote a considerable number of poems, hardly half-a-dozen appeared in print during his lifetime. This is remarkable when we remember that other poets, his contemporaries, probably of poorer quality than Evan published volumes of their work. When he left the home, it was usually to go to an Eisteddfod or a meeting of the Ivorites – there is no suggestion that he ever went to a chapel. Although the one picture of him that has survived suggests a dapper, well-dressed little man, according to Thomas Leyshon he was never really concerned with the cut of his suit. Yet he was respected by all who knew him and he was always warmly welcomed in any company, as an entertaining man and a skilled debater. He spent much of his spare time reading, discussing Welsh literature and writing poetry.

It is obvious that he was encouraged by his father to write poetry, and as has already been noted at least three of his brothers were poets. Daniel Huws in the *National Library of Wales Journal* (Winter 1969) makes a reference to Evan responding to a request from his father for a copy of one of his poems. And there is a hint of parental pride in another of Evan's childish efforts:

> *Bu gennyf ddafad unwaith,*
> *Cadd lond ei bol o fwyd,*
> *Ond, och fi! hon fu farw*
> *Rhwng gwal a phost y glwyd.*
> *Mi wneuthum farwnad iddi*

Er mwyn cael ysgafnhad
I'm hiraeth – mae'r gân honno
Yn rhywle gan fy nhad.

(I had a sheep at onetime,
She was so very well fed,
But, woe me! She died
'Tween gatepost and the wall.
I wrote an elegy for her
In order to get relief
For my grief – that poem is somewhere
In my father's care.)

He was also on good terms with his stepmother. Although references by Thomas T. Leyshon and Daniel Huws suggest that Elizabeth James died sometime after the birth of the last of her children in 1816, the records of Saint Martin's Church, Caerphilly, show that she died on December 3, 1824,

A view that Evan James would have recognised – the Brunel railway bridge across the Rhondda, taken from close to where Evan's factory once stood

and was buried on December 12. If so, the memories of his real mother would not have been those of a young child. Yet he does not mention her with the directness of his references to his stepmother. Did he wish to please his stepmother? We find him praising his upbringing, the good food and a hint that the stepmother spoilt the children behind the father's back. And in one poem Evan says that his stepmother urged him to smoke a pipe to stoke up his muse!

Wrth ffynnon bell y coedca
Mawr y prydyddio fu,
Fy llysfam weithiau'n pipian,
Rôl hynny, wip i'r tŷ.
Hi geisiau fy mherswadio
Y gwnawn brydyddio'n well
Ond cael 'long pipe' i smocio
Gerllaw i dan y gell.

(By the distant well of Coedcae
 The muse would often come,
 My stepmother then came peeping,
 Then popping back indoors!
 At times she then would urge me
 That I would write much better,
 If I had a long-pipe to smoke
 By me at my study!)

Many of his *englynion* reveal a liberal man, sympathetic to his fellow man and supportive of the working classes. He was savage in his criticism of a Justice of the Peace who he evidently believed to have treated someone unfairly in these *englynion* found in his manuscripts at the National Library:

Wele adail y diawledig – ustus
Cestog a mileinig,

Anaddas ŵr boneddig,
Llwyr ddifawl yw y diawl dig.

Oherwydd fod ganddo arian – a thai
A thir, barna weithian
Gall yn hollol, ddyn siolwan,
Wthio i'r gors weithiwr gwan.

(Behold a devilish appearance – a justice
   Corpulent and savage,
Unsuitable noble man
Unpraiseworthy is the wrathful devil.

Because he has money – and houses
   And land, he believes now
That he can completely, miserable man,
Shove into the marsh a weak worker.)

We find him attacking slavery, grieving after Lincoln,
critical of the tithe, praising Garibaldi.

The late Rev W. Rhys Nicholas, very cleverly succeeded
in translating into English an *englyn* Evan had written to
Garibaldi while adhering totally to the strict rules of the
cynghanedd. It is worth reprinting here as it gives those without
an understanding of the language some indication as to the
intricacies of the old Welsh metres.

Build to Garibaldi – an edifice
To defy times stormy,
An institute of beauty
For you are forever free.

His attitude to temperance was interesting. While he
was at the Ancient Druid, Argoed, he was described as a
publican and weaver. One version of the story of the

composition of *Hen Wlad Fy Nhadau* has him calling for a pint of beer from the Colliers Arms for inspiration. If, as D. H. Owen claimed, he never put pen to paper to write a poem without first having a beer, he must have indulged rather a lot, because he was a prolific poet. It is remarkable that the efforts of Ceiriog and Talhaiarn to write an anthem on the air *Glan Medd-dod Mwyn* (The Verge of Sweet Intoxication) were rejected by the Welsh people, yet they accepted an anthem written by two innkeepers – or at least one who had been a publican, and another who went on to be one. He probably held the same view as Myfyr Morganwg – drink was fine, in moderation.

Yet we find him writing an *englyn* in memory of a teetotaller named Samuel Francis:

> *Teilwng lwyr-ymataliwr – i feddwon*
> *Bu'n fuddiol gynghorwr;*
> *Fel pob gonest ddirwestwr*
> *Ei ddiod ef oedd y dŵr.*

> (A worthy teetotaller – to drunkards
> A beneficial adviser;
> Like every honest abstainer
> His only drink was water.)

Where, then, did Evan get his skills as a poet – in particular his understanding of the traditional metres? It has been noted – in the biographical note previously quoted – that his brother, Lewis, had received a good education. Yet, at the age of 13 Lewis was learning his craft as a shoemaker and cobbler. Evan acknowledges the encouragement of his father, mother and stepmother. The Circulating Schools system established by Griffith Jones, Llanddowror, thrived in the Caerphilly area in the mid-18th century. Their aim was to teach people to read, and it is likely that their influence would have continued. Once a member of a family had learned to read that person would pass on that skill to the next generation. Evan mentions that his father, throughout his life, had been a Sunday School teacher. And did he, and his brothers, receive any encouragement from his mother, descendant of the learned and cultured Stradling family? As for poetry there was on the borders of Gwent and Glamorgan a lively literary community. Griffith John Williams in his book on the literary tradition of Glamorgan mentions Lewis Hopkin addressing the poets of Gelligaer in a series of *englynion*, poets who had mastered the old metres and held *cyrddau* – presumably Eisteddfodau – there. This was in 1735. It is not clear whether this tradition continued unbroken, but over a century later there were thriving Eisteddfodau in Gelligaer and Evan and his brother Lewis were playing a prominent part in them.

The Ivorites provided encouragement, but he was writing poetry years before that charitable movement had been founded. Afterwards, the influences of the beliefs and the stimulus of the meetings of the Ivorites are clear on Evan James's poems, both in the traditional and free metres. *Urdd y Gwir Iforiaid* (The Order of True Ivorites) was named after Ifor Hael (circa 1313-1380), Gwernyclepa, Bassaleg, Newport. He was one of Dafydd ap Gwilym's patrons; the poet and antiquarian Evan Evans (Ieuan Brydydd Hir) wrote a series of *englynion* to his ruined court in the 18th century and Iolo Morganwg admired him greatly.

The Order was founded in Wrexham in 1836, and in 1838 the first South Wales branch was opened in Carmarthen. On January 26, 1839, the first lodge in Monmouthshire was founded in The Boot, Cwm Rhydderch, Ebbw Vale, the inn kept by Evan James's brother, Lewis James, and among Evan's diaries there is an ode he wrote to celebrate the occasion. He was, therefore, an early member of the Ivorites, nearly a decade before he came to Pontypridd. The order had a lively lodge in Hopkinstown, Pontypridd, which met at *Y Castell Ifor*, a pub on the banks of the Rhondda where it is claimed that James James sang *Hen Wlad Fy Nhadau* to his own harp accompaniment soon after it was composed. The pub was demolished when the road was widened in the 1970s. The name was

Wetherspoons – Yr Ieuan ap Iago in Aberdare. This should be Yr Iago ap Ieuan, it was James James who lived in Aberdare.

retained and adopted by a non-political club, now a pub, the *Castle Ivor*, on the corner of Foundry Road and Telekiber Street, Hopkinstown – about a quarter of a mile from the site of the original inn.

The Order of Ivorites was a charity providing care for its members and families in times of hardship, illness and death. While charities such as the Oddfellows were run by the middle classes, the Ivorites was a Welsh charity, Welsh in language and working class. They supported the idea of Welsh language education and invariably held an Eisteddfod after their dinners. The poets among the Ivorites were expected to have poem or a song to greet the members at the dinners and Evan James's papers and diaries show that he contributed regularly to these gatherings. By placing such emphasis on participation the Ivorites played an important role as patrons of poets and poetry. Their meetings were lively with much leg pulling – a more formal version of *Clic y Bont*. They had their own journal, *Yr Iforydd*, with its own poetry section which often included poems in praise of the Ivorites – like the following extract from one of Evan James's poems found among his papers, although, to the best of my knowledge, never published –

Mae cenedlgarwch yn tanio'n mynwesau,
Nis gallwn anghofio gorchestion hen oesau,
A wnawn ni ddibrisio iaith bêr ein hynafiaid?
"O na wnawn byth bythoedd," medd pawb o'r Iforiaid!

(Patriotism burns in our bosoms,
We will never forget great deeds of the past,
Will we neglect the sweet tongue of our fathers?
"Never in eternity," say all the Ivorites.)

Evan James belongs in that rich tradition of Welsh social poets, a tradition rooted in the very earliest of Welsh poets reaching its climax in the Middle Ages and still fit and well in the present day. We find him writing many elegies and poems in praise of someone. There is a poem in praise of *"W. Price, Esq, Doctor, Porthyglo, for curing William Jones, Gelligaer, from an illness that caused him pain for a long time"*. It could have been a poem entered for a competition, as poems were invited for the Gelligaer eisteddfod of 1848 in praise of William Price and his work in providing medical care for the coalminers. We can be certain that the subject of Evan's poem was the Dr William Price as he was living in Porthyglo, Pontypridd, at that time. Another poem by Evan gives praise to *"Mr Isaac Thomas, Carpenter"* for providing coffins at a cheap price for the *"working classes"*. We find him writing *englynion* to his friend and neighbour in Mill Street, Aaron Cule, on being elected guardian of Llanwynno parish, April 12, 1869. Again in the tradition of the social poet he records local events. There is a poem on *The Revival that will be brought by the New Railroad in the vicinity of Newbridge* (probably Pontypridd but it could be Goetre'r Coed viaduct) *and Quakers Yard*. Like Tom Paine he has no qualms about praising industry and commerce. The poem is dated 1841, which suggests it was written to celebrate the opening of the Abercynon to Merthyr section of the Taff Vale Railway. The references to coal suggest that he also had in mind the opening, at the same time, of the Quakers Yard to Llancaeach branch line.

> Mor hoff gan wladgarwyr yw gweled arwyddion
> Am gynnydd Masnachaeth trwy gyrrau eu gwlad,
> Ynghyd â mawr lwyddiant anturwyr dewrgalon
> Agorant loweithiau er dirfawr les-had.
> Er bod yng ngrombiliau ein parthau mynyddig
> Ddefnyddiau trafnidiaeth – cyflawnder o lo,
> Tra difudd in' ydyw'r trysorau cuddiedig
> Heb gaffael cyfleustra i'w cludaw drwy'n bro.
> Wi! Lloned y Meistriaid – boed elwch i'r gweithwyr,
> Ceir gweld Cledrffordd newydd, dynesu mae'r dydd,
> Gerllaw y Bontnewydd a Mynwent y Crynwyr
> Er lles cyffredinawl – Adfywiad a fydd.

(How pleasing for patriots to see indications
Of the marching of commerce throughout our land,
As well as successes for stouthearted investors
The opening of collieries for the good of us all.
Although in the depths of our mountainous districts
Lies material for progress – abundance of coal,

There will be no use for these hidden treasures
If we cannot move them throughout our land.
Good cheer to the Masters – let the workers make merry,
We shall see the new railroad, the day does grow near,
Close to the Newbridge and by Quakers Yard
For the good of us all – a revival we'll come.)

There is greater skill in another poem, *The Good Brought By The Woollen Factories of Caerphilly*, with its abundance of rhymes:

Canfyddir hen wragedd a gwlân rhwng ei bysedd,
Er mwyn caffael meinwedd edafedd fo deg,
Y garwaf ddeolant, y tecaf er tyciant
Ddetholant, ni oedant un adeg.

Mae'r gweithiau cysurlon er budd i gribyddion,
I nyddwyr, lliwyddion, gwehyddion tra gwych,
Heb son am niferi o fân-blant sy'n gweini,
Gan brofi'n daioni dianwych.

(Old women are spotted with wool 'tween their fingers,
To make knitting wool, the finest of all,
The roughest they'll discard, the finest provided
Selected, no second is wasted.

The comforting factories for the good of the combers,
The knitters, the dyers, the weavers so skilled,
As well as the numerous children attending,
Profiting from abundance of goodness.)

He wrote poems to *Tredegar's New Steam Engine* (1839), *The Perthigleision Stone Quarry* (1852), *Aberdare Market* (1853),

The New Workhouse for the Poor, Pontypridd (1866) and *Coedpenmaen Works* (1866). Poems that, again, show the influence of the ideas of Tom Paine.

Evan James was an admirable representative of the culture of his district, taking his place comfortably in a society of small farmers and craftsmen. He was thoughtful, a man of independent mind. An interesting and revealing newspaper report exists of a speech he made at the Gelligaer Eisteddfod, Christmas Day 1848 (see appendix 3). His brother, Lewis, was the president and Evan was with him on the stage. In his address Evan speaks of the social responsibilities of the poet and he urges his contemporaries to involve themselves in all branches of literature so that their names will be perpetuated, *"so that posterity may know that once such men had lived and not thrown away their time"*. An exhortation to the working classes to take up their pens – a romantic notion, and yet another suggestion that the ideas of Iolo Morganwg lay heavily on him. He continues and notes that the Welsh, like other nations, have their antiquities and he is pleased that *"his brothers, the English"* always commend and credit the Welsh *Triads* – *"compositions of peculiar ability and wit"*, he noted. So what lay behind these references?

Iolo Morganwg was the first to translate the *Triads* into English in *The Myvyrian Archaiology*, 1801. They were published again, shortly afterwards by Edward Davies in his *Celtic Researches* in 1804, a volume with some wild and weird claims and theories that nevertheless made a deep impression on European poets, such as the French Parnassian poet Leconte de Lisle. In a reprint of his *History of the Anglo-Saxons* – circa 1807 – Sharon Turner wrote at some length about the *Triads* in a substantial appendix, titled *A Vindication of the Ancient British Poems*.

"The Franks, then, had poets – the Saxons had poets – the

Irish had poets. Let us, then, not deny them to the Welsh," wrote Turner in his conclusion to the appendix. Turner is now the forgotten man of English history but for sixty years he was their principle historian, and his book was the standard work on the history of England. It appears that Evan was well acquainted with his work and approved of Iolo Morganwg's view that the English *"brothers"* needed to be enlightened about the history of the original inhabitants of these islands. And that the English should realise and accept that the history of the Welsh and the other Celts is a part of their history, too.

It is not a point of view of great concern to nationalists, but Iolo, during his time in London went to some trouble to get to know and befriend the English and to attempt to teach them something about the history and culture of Wales and the Welsh language.

Towards the end of his speech – or at least the report of it that appears in the *Monmouthshire Merlin* – Evan James announces that a new monthly magazine for women, *Y Gymraes*, is about to appear. To *"loud cheers"* he urges everyone present to subscribe to it, *"inasmuch as there had been such libellous allegations against the character and chastity of the fair sex belonging to Wales"*. That last exhortation was a reference to the report of the commissioners into the state of education in Wales, usually referred to as The Treason of the Blue Books for the way they criticised the lack of education and the morality of the Welsh. The commissioners were three English Anglicans, coming into a Welsh speaking, increasingly non-conformist Wales, unable to converse with schoolchildren in their own language who took the view that the chapels and the Eisteddfodau were at the root of this immorality. I have never seen any proof that Evan ever contributed to the short-lived *Gymraes* although I found among his papers in The National Library a copy of a series of *englynion* he had submitted to it under the pen name of Meudwy Glan Rhondda.

Evidently, Evan James was a man of strong opinions; he was well read and had a deep respect for books. In Pontypridd Museum can be seen his copies of the two volumes of Gweirydd ap Rhys's *Hanes y Brytaniaid a'r Cymry* (History of the British and the Welsh), bound in the best leather. Also in the museum are bound volumes of the 1861 and 1863 editions of *The Controversialist*. Or to give its full title, *The British Controversialist and Literary Magazine devoted to the Impartial and Deliberate Discussion of Important Questions in Religion, Philosophy, History, Politics, Social Economy &c and to the Promotion of Self-culture and General Education.* It was a freethinking journal discussing in great depth and detail such topics as *Polish Independence From the Russian Empire; Is The House Of Lords Beneficial To The Country? Is The Permanent Connection Of The British Colonies With The Mother Country Desirable? Do We Need Ministers?* It contained articles on scientific subjects such as one on James Watt and the – not very rapid – utilization of steam power. The topics investigated in this journal are often reflected in his poems. He writes about slavery. Making public spectacles of such feats as walking the tightrope was a subjected discussed in the journal. Evan writes an *englyn*, admittedly not a very serious one, to Blondin. And his positive views towards industry.

Evan emerges as a man who held pacifist views. *Diddichell, da heddychwr* (Without malice, a good pacifist) wrote ap Myfyr in one of his *englynion* in memory of Evan James. He would have been in agreement with the opinions of Myfyr and others of the Rocking Stone *Gorsedd*. In the chapter *An Attempt to Revive Druidism at Pontypridd* in his *History of Pontypridd and District*, Morien gives an interesting description of an event held at the Rocking Stone *"around 1853"*.

According to Morien, who admits to relying on his childhood memory "(Myfyr) had small posters distributed throughout Pontypridd announcing that at the next Sunday nearest the Summer Solstice (June 21), a prophecy spoken by Isaiah 3,000 years ago would be fulfilled on the Pontypridd Rocking Stone. This excited great curiosity, for however much Myfyr might be mistaken about religion, no one doubted his veracity and earnestness." On that Sunday the crowds gathered in their hundreds, but there was no sign of the Prophet Isaiah, only Myfyr, followed by "*his acolytes*" carrying two white poles, ascended the Rocking Stone. After Myfyr had offered a prayer, a hymn was sung to the accompaniment of the harp

> *Cyn codi allorau na themlau,*
> *Nac urddo offeiriad di-fudd;*
> *Cyn llunio yr ofergoeliaethau*
> *Sydd heddiw yn t'wyllu ein dydd*

> (Before raising up altars and temples,
> And ordaining useless priests;
> Before the creation of the superstitions
> That today darken our day.)

Then the "*acolytes*" with their poles step forward and stand with their poles, one on each side of Myfyr. "I have long felt sympathy with the Prophet Isaiah," said Myfyr. "He was a very able Bard. He was moreover an advocate of universal peace. He was in sympathy with us, for does he not state: 'How beautiful upon the mountain are the feet of Him who bringeth good tidings that proclaimeth peace.'

"But, to this day, after soldiers have butchered thousands of each other, the Clergy gather together and sing 'Te Deum Laudamus' or 'We Praise Thee O God'. We do not worship Saturn and his day here. We adore the Father and Mother of all mankind." The response was *sensational*, according to Morien.

Then Myfyr returned to Isaiah. The Prophet had seen a vision, wrote Morien "a Kingdom of universal rule, with its flag white and the blessed word 'Peace' as the national motto inscribed in gold letters upon it, and with the emblem of a white dove on the pole." Then Myfyr quoted from the Book of Isaiah "... and they shall have beat their swords into ploughshares, and their spears into pruning hooks." Then the acolytes uncovered the tops of their poles and dangling from them were ploughshares and pruning hooks; and Myfyr cried out "Behold! Swords converted into ploughshares, and spears into pruning hooks!" Some laughed, according to Morien, but others applauded warmly. What could have been the significance of that strange ceremony? Morien offers no suggestion. Could it have been a protest against the Crimean War, which began in 1854? Morien is imprecise as to the year when Myfyr held this spectacle at the Rocking Stone, but even if he was correct that it was held in 1853 there had been rumblings and protests against what was, at first, "a popular war". We could be fairly sure that Evan James would have been present at this event. It would seem also that this, and maybe other similar messages, had had their effect. Pontypridd at this time was not fertile ground for military recruitment.

As has already been suggested the Druidic Deism of the Unitarian Iolo Morganwg appears to have been acceptable even with its hints of Druidism as a source of Christianity. Myfyr Morganwg appears to have taken a step too far with his theory that Druidism was the basis of all religions. He was frequently embroiled in debates in the Welsh language press. He responded furiously, for example, to a series of articles on

Iolo Morganwg by Thomas Stephens, the chemist and literary historian, in Yr Ymofynydd (The Inquirer), the journal of the Unitarians. The Rev Edward Roberts, D.D., Minister of Tabernacle, denounced the "infidels posturing as new Welsh Druids" at the Rocking Sone. Not an accusation to be taken lightly in those times.

But there were other happenings at the Rocking Stone that could have been causing great dismay to the Reverend Roberts and other ministers in the Pontypridd area, not least that they were not reaping the fruits of the 1859 revival. A seemingly innocuous report on an Eisteddfod held at the Rocking Stone on June 21st appeared in The Cambrian newspaper of July 6, 1860. Interspersed by harp music by James James three lectures were delivered from the Rocking Stone, two in Welsh and one in English. Of the actual content of the lectures there is no indication, expect that all were eloquent and well received. Even the titles, superficially, are not inspiring. William John (Mathonwy) spoke on Man, The Highest Development in Nature; Gwilym Llancarfan, gave a lecture in English on Geology; and T. ab Iago, gave a lecture on The Benefits Derived at Eisteddfodau by Expanding Knowledge and Morality. The last speaker may have been Tomos ab Iago (Thomas James), youngest brother of Evan James, whose name appears in connection with the Llanover Arms and the Orpheus (James James) collection of airs submitted to the 1858 Llangollen Eisteddfod. But Mathonwy's lecture, coming one year after the publication of Charles Darwin's Origin of Species, would appear to have been a lecture discussing and in support of the new theory. A red rag to the Creationists! Gwilym Llancarfan's lecture appears not to have been a technical talk for men digging for coal. Geologists were the first people to disprove the Creationist assertion that the world was formed 4000 years ago. The T. ap

Iago lecture reflected a view, gaining acceptance in some circles, that Christianity was not the only provider of standards of morality – there was a scientific basis for morality, too. Lectures on subjects such as these would not have received the approval of the chapels of the time. Wales may have been the one country in Western Europe to become more religious as it became more industrialised. If that is so, Pontypridd was well out of step with the rest of Wales!

Evan James, although living most of his life within close proximity to Merthyr and Aberdare, was born and brought up in communities that were still to a large extent pre-industrial. Even the years he spent in Pontypridd were before the town experienced its huge wave of inward migration. His life spanned the rural and the industrial, experiencing more than one way of life, more than one form of society, one that was Welsh speaking but becoming less so. He was steeped in the old poetic tradition and participated in it; he found inspiration and ideas in Welsh history and the misty Druidism of ancient times. Yet he was open to new progressive ideas. But he will be remembered for one song that crystallised the growing national consciousness and pride of his people.

Anthem of the Bretons

Not only have we, the Welsh, been inspired by the anthem composed by the father and son from Pontypridd, so, too, have our Celtic brothers and sisters, the Bretons and the Cornish. As the ancient Brythonic Celts travelled from Wales and Cornwall to Brittany in the early centuries of Christianity, so did *Hen Wlad Fy Nhadau* in the 19th century. And if the music caused controversy in Wales in 1884, it was the words that stirred up trouble Brittany.

In 1897 W. Jenkyn Jones (1852-1925), a Welsh Protestant missionary in Quimper, southern Brittany, published a volume of Breton hymns with the title *Telen ar C'hristen* (The Christian's Harp). Jenkyn Jones, from New Quay, Ceredigion, had been a schoolteacher, then in 1880 he went as a missionary to Brittany where he lived until his death in 1925. A number of Welshmen went to Brittany as Protestant missionaries around this time. Many of the people of western Brittany were monoglot Breton speakers at this time and the Welsh-speaking missionaries who came in their midst soon learnt the language. Jenkyn Jones did so and before long he was writing poetry in Breton. His book of hymns, *Telen ar C'hristen,* contains a number of translations of popular Welsh hymns and among them is a hymn he wrote to be sung to the tune of *Hen Wlad Fy Nhadau.* The two first verses, to all intents and purposes, are translations of, and in the spirit of the original. After that the hymn becomes more religious. It chastises the drink and the fourth verse calls on the Bretons to free themselves from their captivity – presumably the Catholic Church – and to proclaim the name of Jesus for the progress of the true faith. These are the first three verses:

Doue ha va Bro

Peb Breizad tomm-galon a gâr, sûr, he vro,
Bro Arvor 'zo brudet dre'r bed tro-var-dro;
Er brezel calonnec, hon tadou ervad,
A seuliaz evithi ho gwad.

O va mamm-bro! Cared a rann va bro,
Keit mat vo'r môr 'vel mur en dro,
Ra vezo libr atao va bro.

Bretoned, tud caled, 'vel dero int creñv,
N'euz bro 'vel Breiz-Izel a-zindan an env;
Peb menez, pep traouien a garomp ervad,
Hon tadou ho livaz a wad.

O va mamm-bro &c.

Gwin ardant 'zo tirant da veur a zen foll
He spered, he galon, he gorf en eun taol
P'ar monstr en e'selavach zo gwerzet 'vel preiz
P'int stlapomp ar monstr euz a Vreiz.

O va mamm-bro &c.

(Translation)

God and my Country

Every warm-hearted Breton who loves his land,
This land of Brittany renowned through the world;
So brave in their battles, their fathers absolute,
And for it they spilt their blood.

Oh! My motherland, I love my country,
May the sea be a strong wall around it,
So that our country is free forever.

Bretons, stout nation, oak-like in strength,
There is no land like Brittany so highly respected,
Every mountain, every valley, we love completely.
Our fathers coloured it with their blood.

Oh! My motherland &c

The hot wine is king of the strong and the foolish,
His spirit, his heart, his body will fall
Underfoot of the monster who cheats all by treason;
Let's exile the enemy from our land.

Oh! My motherland &c

The trouble arose when another translation emerged soon after, by the young Breton poet Taldir (Fañch Jaffrennou, 1879-1956). As can be seen, it is very similar to Jenkyn Jones's translation – except that Taldir, by trade a wine merchant, omitted all references to temperance.

Bro goz ma zadou

Ni, Breiziz a galon, karomp hon gwir Vro!
Brudet en an Arvor dre ar bed tro-dro.
Dispont kreiz ar brezel, hon zadou ken mad
A skuillaz eviti o gwad.

O Breiz! Ma bro, me gar ma bro;
Tra ma vo mor 'vel mur 'n he zro
A vezo digabestr ma bro!

Breiz, douar ar Zent coz, douar ar Varzed,
N'eus bro all a garan kement 'barz ar bed.
Pob menez, pob trauoien d'am c'halon zo ker:
Enne kousk meur a Vreizad ter.

O Breiz! &c

Ar Vretoned a zo tud kaled ha kreñv;
N'eus pobl ken kalonek a-zindan an env,
Gwerz trist, zon dudius a ziwan eno.
O pegent kaer ec'h out, ma Bro.

O Breiz! &c

Mar d'eo bet trec'het Breiz er brezelliou braz,
He iez a zo bepred ken beo ha biskoaz;
He c'halon birvidik a lamm c'hoaz 'n he c'hreiz,
Dihunet out breman, ma Breiz.

O Breiz! &c

(Translation)

Old Land of my Fathers

We stouthearted Bretons, we love our true land!
*Arvor is famous through the world.
Fearless in battle, our bravest fathers
Spilt their blood.

Oh! Brittany! I love my land.
While the sea forms a wall around it
May there be freedom for my country!

(*Arvor or Armor is an ancient name for Brittany)

Brittany, soil of the Saints, land of the Bards,
There is no other land I love so much in the world.
Every mountain, every valley are dear to my heart:
From its deep sleep it will effortlessly wake.

Oh! Brittany! &c

The Bretons are a nation hard and strong;
There are none braver under heaven.
The sad ballads, sweet songs that it guards.
So lovely are you, my land!

Oh! Brittany! &c

If Brittany was defeated in great battles,
Its language is always as alive as ever;
Its fervent heart leaps in her breast.
Wake now this hour, my Brittany!

Oh! Brittany! &c

The Welsh writer Ambrose Bebb knew Jenkyn Jones
and Taldir and there is a chapter on each of them in his book
Pererindodau (Pilgrimages). Bebb, diplomatically, described
Taldir's words as a re-working of Jenkyn Jones's translation
but there was *"more of the spirit of the original"* in Taldir's song
– which seems a fair assessment.

Bro Goz ma Zadou has been accepted as the national
anthem of Brittany since 1902 and in 2003 a plaque was
unveiled in the square of the town of Lesneven, a town
twinned with Carmarthen, to celebrate that centenary. The
town's lycée is also twinned with Ysgol Gyfun Gymraeg
Rhydfelen, Pontypridd, and Ysgol Bro Myrddin, Carmarthen.

There have been translations of Hen Wlad Fy Nhadau
into every one of the Celtic languages and there have been

attempts to have it accepted as an anthem of the Celtic nations, but as far as I know it is only in Brittany and Cornwall that it is sung regularly. Two Cornish translations exist, the first by Gwas Mihal (Henry Jenner, 1848-1934) and the second by Mordon (Robert Morton Nance, 1873-1959). Both had Welsh connections, the Jenner family with Wenvoe Castle – Jenner Park, Barry, was named after a member of the same family - and Mordon was born in Cardiff. The following poem is Mordon's Cornish translation followed by the translations into the other Celtic languages:

Bro Goth Agan Tasow

Bro goth agan Tasow, dha fleghes a'th car,
Gwlas ker an Howlsedhas, pan vro yu dha bar,
War oll an norvys 'th on-ny scullyes ales,
Mes agan kerenza yu dhys.

Kernow! Kernow! Y keryn Kernow;
An mor hedra vo yn fos dhys adro,
'Th on 'Onen hag oll' rag Kernow.

Irish

Sean-tír Mo Shínsear

'S í sean-tír mo shinsear is ionmhuin le m'chroidhe
Tír bárd as tir ceoltóíf is mó clú as brigh,
A laocha 's tréin-fhir fíor-chalma le tlás
Chum saoirseachta chuaidh siad trén bás.

Sean-tír! Is tusa is mó le mo chroidhe
Chom fada 's beidheas monubhar na toinne le d'chuan,
Bidheadh againn an Gaedhilg go buan.

Scots Gaelic

Dùthaich Mo Shinnsire

A dhùthaich mo shinnsire', a dhùthaich mo ghaoil
Sàr-mhuime nam bàrd thu, is màthair nan laoch,
Nan curaidhean treubach a dh' éirich 'gad dhion
'S a dhòirteadh am fuil anns an strì.

Shean-tir mo ghaoil, 's tu mo dhachaidh gu fìor
Cho fhad 's a bhios farum na tuinne ri d'thìr
A dhùthaich, a thasgaidh mo chridh'.

Manx

Heer my Hennayraghyn

O Heer my Hennayraghyn, Heer my chree hene,
Voir ghraihagh dy vardyn ta greinnaghey shin.
As treanee nagh lhig da dty ard-ghoo goll ersooyl
Son seyrsnys ren deayrtey nyn vuill.

Vannin! O ta my chree lhiat hene,
Choud's vees y keayn
Nee dty hraieyn niee,
Bee'n cree aym rhyts firrinagh dy beayn.

The Memorial in the Park

In the years after James James's death in 1902 there was a campaign to build a memorial to the composers of *Hen Wlad Fy Nhadau*. But there was not much money around and then came The Great War and it was not until 1930 that a memorial, worthy of the achievement of Evan and James James, was erected in Ynysangharad Park, Pontypridd. Sir William Goscombe John's splendid memorial, on a plinth of blue stone from Craig-yr-Hesg quarry, was unveiled by Lord Treowen before 10,000 people.

W. Goscombe John (1860-1952) was the son of a Cardiff engraver and sculptor and as a teenager had worked with his father creating wooden carvings to the specifications of William Burgess who was building Cardiff Castle for the Third Marquis of Bute. Although he was 21 before he embarked on his formal education as an artist and sculptor he became one of Britain's most important official sculptors of the first half of the 20th century. His works can be found in far-flung corners of the old British Empire. He played a prominent part in establishing a National Museum for Wales, and a number of his works can be seen in the museum, together with a statue of Saint David in Cardiff's City

The Memorial in Ynysangharad Park

125

Hall. Among his other works is the memorial to Caradog in Aberdare, and the Horn for the National Eisteddfod *Gorsedd*. He also produced a bust of Sydney Curnow Vosper, artist of the iconic Welsh painting *Salem*. That bust is in Cyfarthfa Castle Museum, Merthyr.

The memorial to Evan and James James takes the form of two sculptures, one of a young man the other a young woman, one representing the muse, the other music. Beneath are images of the father and son *"who inspired a deep and tender love of their native land united poetry to song and gave to Wales her national hymn Hen Wlad Fy Nhadau"*.

It is interesting to note that the image of Evan James, in all probability faces the wrong way, as his photograph was once developed from the wrong side of a negative. Goscombe John cannot be blamed for this. A number of similar photographs exist having been developed in the same way, even pen-and-ink sketches of Evan based on these wrong-way-round prints.

Images of James and Evan James on the Memorial

The statue is one of the better public monuments of Wales. It also stands in one of the most delightful parks in South Wales surrounded by hills with such lovely names as Y Graig, Coed-y-Wion, Y Graigwen, Coed-y-lan, Craig-yr-Hesg, Coedpenmaen and Craig-yr-Helfa.

In the 1950s the grave of Evan and Elizabeth James was found to be in a state of neglect, the gravestone had been vandalised and the cemetery of Carmel Chapel overgrown with weeds. One of the chapel deacons, a Scot named W. T. H. Gilmour, began a campaign to tidy the cemetery and create a Memorial Garden. Two ministers from Ton Pentre, the Rev T. Alban Davies and the Rev L. Haydn Lewis, and the Director of the Welsh youth organisation, Urdd Gobaith Cymru, R. E. Griffith, who was himself from Cilfynydd, met at the 1963 Llanelli National Eisteddfod and joined the campaign. But in 1969, before the plans had come to fruition, the council announced that it was going to widen the road, Carmel Chapel was knocked down and any hope of a Memorial Garden had gone. Then came the suggestion to exhume the remains of Evan and Elizabeth James to be re-buried in Ynysangharad Park by the Memorial. The damaged gravestone was repaired and the re-burial took place on July 1, 1973, with a service officiated by the Rev Haydn Lewis, Ton Pentre, and the Rev D. Emlyn Lewis, Minister of Tabernacl, Pontypridd. On the gravestone are the words:

Er Cof Hiraethlawn Am
Evan James,
"Ieuan ap Iago", Pontypridd,
yr hwn a fu farw, Medi y 30ain 1878, yn 69 mlwydd oed
(In Grieving Memory For
Evan James
"Ieuan ap Iago", Pontypridd,
who died, September 30th 1878, aged 69)

There follows a *hir-a-thoddaid* (eight line stanza in traditional metre) written by ap Myfyr, the son of Myfyr Morganwg, who had initiated Evan into the Rocking Stone Gorsedd on June 21, 1850.

Evan James's grave in Ynysangharad Park

Yn y bedd isod mae un bydd oesau
'N uchel ganmawl ei haeddiannawl ddoniau,
Fel awenydd ac un o filiynau,
Ein IEUAN ydoedd, a'i fyw syniadau
Unig-anedig yn ei ganiadau
Enaid-lwythog, a chan genhedlaethau
E gludir 'n eu treigladau – glod y gŵr
A fu yn awdwr Hen Wlad Fy Nhadau.

(In the grave below is one for whom generations
Will give praise for his meritorious talents,
As a man of the muse and one in a million,
He was our IEUAN with his lively ideas
Unique in his songs
Which are heavy of soul, and by generations
Shall be borne in their meanderings – praise for the man
Who was the author of Hen Wlad Fy Nhadau.)

Poems by Evan James

Evan James was a prolific poet who appears to have written almost exclusively for his own amusement. This is a very brief selection from a formidable mass of hitherto unpublished work, an attempt to give some indication of his interests, his opinions and sympathies. These include Druidism, Industry, Poverty, Patriotism and the Language. He wrote a huge number of englynion – the four-line poems in the traditional Welsh metres. Some of these have already been included in a previous chapter, along with translations. The only poem in the old metres in this section is the one praising Dr William Price.

Apart from one poem - *A Patriotic Song – Give Me a Cottage* – I have confined myself to quoting just one verse of the original, but the translations are included in full. The reason for including *A Patriotic Song* in its entirety is that the second verse contains the "missing" ten lines of what has been suggested is the original version of *Hen Wlad Fy Nhadau.*

Y Derwydd

Ar fore teg tan ael y bryn
Canfyddais dderwydd barfog syn
Yn tremio'n athrist tua'r glyn.
Anturiais ofyn iddaw:
"O Dderwydd, gysegredig wedd
A barcha'r gwir, a feithrin hedd,
Ar foncyff crin pam gwnei dy sedd
Mewn prudd unigedd distaw?"

TRANSLATION

The Druid

One morning, on the sloping brow,
I saw a Druid, long his beard,
Staring sadly at the vale.
I ventured asking him:
"Oh Druid, holy of countenance,

129

Truthful, respectful, loving peace,
Why, sadly on this withered log
You sit in lonely silence?"

"My son," replied the goodly man,
"The blood flows wildly in my veins
Perceiving prejudice and treason,
Decline in the muse's land.
What evil to our nation did
I, that it abuses me,
For worshipping beneath the oak
With clear conscience?

"Numerous the libels and contempt
- Futile efforts to find fault
And uproot ancient Druidism -
Flow from the press's womb.
To see the dawn of ancient times
- Better then a thousand times -
Before dark, foul fanaticism
Bound us in treachery.

"The charm of our children's games,
The thunder of cascading streams,
The surging storm amidst the peaks
Are signs of freedom all.
And if honestly I try
To raise a cry in freedom's cause
My persecutors cause me pain
Raised in a savage voice.

"And without fear will I face
The libel of the murmuring men,
And Lilliputian giants will
Flee from the pure truth.
Moral lessons so profound
Seen in the stars, among the leaves;
By the Creator's endless power
Manifest in nature's beauty.

"When wandering in the light of day
Such wonder do I then perceive
Among the gentle, tender flowers
In nature's bounteous fields.
And when the night pulls down its veil
From these I then shall cast mine eyes
To wonder at the heaven's lamps
In Ceridwen's exquisite court.

(This poem, from the National Library of Wales Evan James MSS, appears to have been written around 1856. Reports in the Welsh language press show that Myfyr Morganwg and John Williams (ab Ithel) had responded to disparaging comments about their activities at the Rocking Stone. Whether Druidism in general was under attack, the Druids of the Rocking Stone were certainly coming in for criticism. Evan James, here, springs to the defence of his fellow Druids. The poem was written to be sung to the tune Ar Fore Teg [On a Fine Morning].)

Cân yr Adfywiad

(Ar Agor y Gledrffordd newydd yng Nghymdogaeth y Bontnewydd a Mynwent y Crynwyr)

Mor hoff gan wladgarwyr yw gweled arwyddion
Am gynnydd Masnachaeth trwy gyrrau eu gwlad,
Ynghyd â mawr lwyddiant anturwyr dewrgalon
Agorant lo-weithiau er dirfawr lesâd.
Er bod yng ngrombiliau ein parthau mynyddig
Ddefnyddiau trafnidiaeth – cyflawnder o lo,
Tra difudd i'n ydyw'r trysorau cuddiedig
Heb gaffael cyfleustra i'w cludo drwy'n bro.
Wi! Lloned y meistriaid – boed elwch i'r gweithwyr,
Ceir gweld cledrffordd newydd, dynesu mae'r dydd,
Gerllaw y Bontnewydd a Mynwent y Crynwyr
Er llês cyffredinol – adfywiad a fydd.

TRANSLATION

The Revival

The Revival – or Renewal - that will come as a result of the New Railroad
in the vicinity of Newbridge and Quakers Yard

How pleasing for patriots to see indications
As commerce comes marching throughout our land,
As well as successes for stout-hearted investors
The opening of collieries for the good of us all.
Although in the depths of our mountainous districts
Lies material for progress – abundance of coal,
How useless will be those hidden treasures
If we cannot move them throughout our land.
Good cheer to the Masters – let the workers make merry,
The day of the railroad it comes ever nearer,
Close to the Newbridge and by Quakers Yard;
For the good of us all – a revival there'll be.

Strive your hardest, you labouring workers,
Despite all obstructions, to cut through the hills.
The need it is pressing, we all are impatient
To see our railway completed so soon.
You who are owners of coalfields abundant
Awake, the time it will rapidly come,
And then you'll be selling your minerals so fine
For your own profits and benefits for all
The echoing whistle of the fast-moving engines
As if to invite those hidden materials
To come up from the depths of the hills to the open
And carried for profit throughout our land.

While I ponder around me, close by the new bridge
And at Quaker's Yard, so happy I feel,
But how greater the pleasure when I view the revival
On the banks of Nant Bargoed and the vale of the Taff?
Coal being sold throughout our district,
Demands for the workforce to dig in the depths
For all that black gold to nourish our trade -
Succourer of virtue so sweet it will be.

The woods will be felled, the stumps will be uprooted
To cut a deep path across our moors
And then will be built such pretty new houses
To be owned by the workers close by to their jobs.

O what a revival, our commerce expanding,
This will encourage the many who own
The wealth, to use for the good of us all
And build all the houses – much profit there'll be;
The shops nearby brimful of those things
Which the railway will bring here so swiftly and cheap;
Rich in their sustenance for all our people
With necessary nourishment for health and for good.
On summery evenings the neighbours will wander
Together, for leisure on the sides of the hill,
Content as they listen to the laughter of children
Who come there to play, ringing out through the vale.

Below all the crags in those desolate places
Paths out of wilderness so soon will be seen,
Where once grew the thistles, the thorns and the brambles
Through hard work and effort improvement will come;
Where now grow the reeds, and the bushes of gorse
Are spreading destruction – we'll all be enjoying
A view so much finer, gardens in flower
And fruits from the trees for everyone's health.
And may success smile on all those who live there
True union and love will bloom in their midst,
For all they will profit, and the good of their workers
A revival in learning and culture for all.

(The Bontnewydd / Newbridge in this poem is probably Pontypridd, and
the poem anticipates the opening the Taff Vale Railway from Abercynon to
Merthyr, the section opened in 1841, the year the poem was written
according to the date in the NLW Evan James MSS.)

Ymweliad Offeiriad â'i Blwyfoges Gystuddiol

Aeth hen offeiriad duwiol, rhyw dro i ofyn hynt
Hen Lowri dlawd gystuddiol o ardal Bwlch-y-gwynt,
Prysurodd yn ei ymdaith ar gefn ei gaseg gref
Rhag ofn i'r henwraig farw cyn cael ei fendith ef.

Rôl mynd i mewn i'r bwthyn a chael rhyw fath o sedd,
Edrychodd mewn tosturi ar Lowri wael ei gwedd
Gan ddweud: "Er eich cysuro mi ddeuthum gyda nwyf
Yn unol â dyledswydd, gweinidog pena'r plwyf."

TRANSLATION

A Vicar Visits a Sick Parishioner

An old and pious vicar, one day went forth to see
Poor Lowri who was sickly nearby to Bwlch-y-gwynt,
He hurried on his journey riding his sturdy mare
In case the woman perished unblessed by a priest.

Once inside the cottage he found a place to sit,
He then looked down at Lowri - so poorly was she -
And said: "So I can give some comfort I hurried to your home,
Which is the proper duty of the parish's foremost priest."

Lowri:
"To you I am so grateful, if my brother you will be,
Generous and kindly to a sickly one like me.
My eighteen pence a week it is not very much,
I was told I would get thirty from the Union in my plight."

Vicar:
"Don't be materialistic, I came along to you
With nourishment spiritual, to help you on your way!"

Lowri:
"After I get your blessing, what good is that to me?
I'd rather half a guinea of cheer in my hand!"

Vicar:
"Please be understanding, it's not money that I give,
It's you I wish to save, from your sinful ways."

Lowri:
"You would be miserable also, despite your belly and mouth,
If your body kept on moving non-stop for fourteen days!"

Vicar:
"Satan has knit his nets ready along our paths,
And sinful is your heart, filthy and very bad!"

Lowri:
"It's not my heart that's bad, sir, you have mistook the place,
The pain is in my shoulder and aching down my side."

Vicar:
"My heart is bleeding for you within your poor abode,
With darkness you're inflicted on this miserable bed."

Lowri:
"With straw I stuffed the windows to keep out wind and snow
That's why this place is darker than the insides of a cow."

Vicar:
I wish I could convince you of your inconsiderations great,
It's obvious your earthly hovel will soon come tumbling down."

Lowri:
"For once I must agree, I'm worried that it will,
Scraping away the foundations, you see, are Twm Shon's hens."

Vicar:
"I see no point in staying, it's better I should leave,
I hold no hopes of saving you from a fiery end!"

Lowri:
"Who wants you to stay here, you could have earlier gone,
There's never been a false one, like you, in Bwlch-y-gwynt!"

(From the NLW, Evan James MSS. The poem is dated June 11, 1863. It is typical of a number of his poems on the subject of poverty and unfortunate people. He also wrote many poems in dialogue form – probably to be sung although he does not suggest a tune for this.)

Penillion o Fawl i William Price

(Yswain, Meddyg, Porthyglo, am ei gywreinrwydd effeithiol yn lleihau y dolur hir a dirdynnol a flinodd William Jones, Gelligaer)

Yng Ngelligaer gwelwyd gŵr llwyd tan gur llym
Fu'n goddef hir fisoedd nes roedd yn ddi-rym,
Sef William Jones, glowr, ei gyflwr oedd gaeth,
Tan bwys ei fawr orthrwm yn wargrwm yr aeth.
Cyffuriau'n ddieffaith – anobaith yn awr,
Cynyddodd ei ddolur trwm hirgur tra mawr.

TRANSLATION

Verses in Praise of William Price

(Doctor, Porthyglo, for his effective skills in easing the long and excruciating pains suffered by William Jones, Gelligaer)

In Gelligaer a pale man was suffering sharp pains
Who suffered many months until he was weak,
Namely William Jones, collier, his condition was bad,
Under the weight of his oppression he stooped in his pain.
The pills they were useless – he could only despair,
As the pain he was suffering daily got worse.

Renew yourself, muse, for the news to proclaim
Of our meritorious doctor to sing his praise
Namely William Price, Esquire, fine noble man,
Wondrous his medicine to the sick of our land;
By the skill of his hand he restored back to health
And to bliss our weakly and miserable man.

Of respect for his efforts for the sick everywhere
Our Esquire deserves the praise of us all.
He understands causes and cures disease
And how to dispense medicines, and never to fail.
Thanks to this knowledge there was noble good
To many who were sickly and poorly of hue.

(The subject of this poem was the famous Dr William Price, Llantrisant, who lived in Porthyglo, Pontypridd, in 1848 when this poem was written. This poem, from the NLW Evan James MSS, may have been submitted to a competition to write a poem in praise of Price's work in the Gelligaer Eisteddfod of 1848. If so, Evan was unsuccessful, the winner was Thomas Williams, Twm Cilfynydd. Evan James was particularly skilled in the old Welsh metres and from a metric point of view this is a sophisticated piece, every line in the poem (not in the translation!) rhymes internally and has echoing consonants. Every line is in *cynghanedd*, but he only uses *cynghanedd sain* e.g.:

Yng Ngelligaer gwel**wyd** g**ŵr** *ll***wyd** tan gur *ll*wm

Y Brodyr sydd Bell

Mor drwm ac hiraethlon ffarwelio â ffrind
 A fyddo'n ymadael â'i wlad,
Cans nid oes un gwrthrych â'i rhwystra rhag mynd
 Ac yntau a'i fryd ar wellâd.
Mi wn am y teimlad, ffrwyth cariad doeth cry,
 Er alaeth, er wylo, pa well?
O eigion fy nghalon, dymunaf yn hy
 Mawr lwyddiant i'r brodyr sydd bell.

TRANSLATION

The Brothers in Exile

It's heavy with grief that we part with our friends
 When they take leave of their land,
Because there is nothing that will stop them going
 As they seek for a better life.
I know well the feeling, the chains of our love;
 Why should I grieve and weep?
From the depths of my heart, I wish them the best
 And success to my brothers afar.

Although they departed and left behind loved ones
 Their relatives and family back home,
May they all prosper and enjoy success
 Our brothers, their children and wives.

On the wings of my fancy I fly with great ease
    Across oceans and leave my small cell,
My brotherly bosom can only wish well
    And comfort to our brothers afar.

(One of Evan James's poems to his brothers who emigrated to America.
NLW, Evan James MSS. He notes that the poem was written on the
shortest day, 1839, along with the word Druid, indicating that he lived in
the Ancient Druid Inn, Argoed.)

Cân Iforaidd

Cymry ffyddlon ydym ni
    Dros ein gwlad a thros ei bri,
Cyndyn deithiwn ddydd ein gwledd
    Mewn brawdgarwch pur a hedd.
O cyd-orfoleddwn, cyd-ymderchwn y dydd
Dan faner Iforiaeth, Iforiaeth a fydd.

TRANSLATION

A Song for the Ivorites

Welsh patriots all are we
    For our country and its fame,
Stubbornly marching on our day
    In pure brotherly peace.
Let us rejoice, and strive this day
Under the banner of Ivorites, Ivorites we'll be.

Let there be no enmity
    To the Order of Ifor Hael,
There's none who does not know the worth
    Of true union and its strength.
Let us rejoice &c.

Who will say that we're not wise
    Helping one another;
Widows and orphans we do find
    Singing our praise.
Let us rejoice &c.

Although many will predict
   The death of our ancient tongue,
It's sweet tones always will be heard
   While true Ivorites exist.
Let us rejoice &c.

(From one of Evan James's accounts books, Museum of Welsh Life, St
Fagan's. The poem is dated July 11, 1876. These words were probably
written to be sung although Evan did not name a tune.)

Cân Wladgarol – O Rhowch i Mi Fwth

Mae llawer yn llwyddo 'nôl myned ymhell
Tros foroedd i wledydd estronol,
Ond mwy ar ôl myned yn methu gwneud gwell
Er siomiant yn eithaf hiraethol.
  Fy ngwlad, o fy ngwlad, pa Gymro a'th âd
  Heb deimlo ei fron yn glwyfedig –
  O rhowch i mi fwth a thelyn neu grwth
  Yn rhywle yng Nghymru fynyddig.

Os nad yw'r hen Gymru fu unwaith mewn bri
Yn awr yn mwynhau ei holl freiniau,
Arafwn ychydig, dywedwch i mi,
Pa wlad sy dan haul heb ei beiau?
  Fy ngwlad, o fy ngwlad, rhof i ti fawrhad
  Dy enw sy'n dra chysegredig –
  O rhowch i mi fwth a thelyn neu grwth
  Yn rhywle yng Nghymru fynyddig.

Cysegrwyd ei bryniau a'i dolydd tra heirdd
Â gwaed ein gwladgarol gyndeidiau;
Llochesodd derwyddon heddychol a beirdd
Rhag difrod yng nghelloedd y creigiau.
  Fy ngwlad, o fy ngwlad, ei noddwyr difrad
  Ddyrchafant eu heniaith gyntefig.
  O rhowch i mi fwth a thelyn neu grwth
  Yn rhywle yng Nghymru fynyddig.

TRANSLATION

A Patriotic Song – Give Me a Cottage

There are many who succeed by travelling afar
O'er oceans to foreign lands,
But many having gone find no prosperity
Are disappointed and long for their home.
My land, Oh! My land, what Welshman will leave you
Without feeling his bosom is pained –
O give me a cottage, a harp or a fiddle
Somewhere in mountainous Wales.

If ancient Wales that once enjoyed fame
No longer enjoys all its privileges,
Just pause for a moment, tell me,
What country beneath the sun that is faultless?
My land, Oh! My Land, I pledge you my honour
Your name is sacred to me -
O give me a cottage, a harp or a fiddle
Somewhere in mountainous Wales.

Its hills and its beautiful dales have been sanctified
With the blood of our patriotic ancestors
The peaceful druids and poets sought refuge
From destruction in the cells midst the rocks.
My land, Oh! My land, its steadfast patrons
Exalt our ancient tongue.
O give me a cottage, a harp or a fiddle
Somewhere in mountainous Wales.

(This poem is of interest because the second verse is the "missing" ten lines
of the original *Hen Wlad Fy Nhadau*. Although these are eight line verses,
they are as quoted by Gweirydd ap Rhys in his *Hanes y Brytaniaid a'r Cymry*
(The History of the Welsh and the Britons). The line splits in the chorus
have been changed thus shortening this version into eight lines. Otherwise
the verses, apart from their form, are identical. From the NLW Evan James
MSS.)

Appendices

Appendix 1

Letter by Taliesin James from his home in 281 Albany Road, Cardiff, dated December 4, 1910, to John Crockett, Pontypridd:

Dear Mr Crockett,

Replying to your enquiry as to when *"Hen Wlad Fy Nhadau"* was composed, I have before me the original manuscript of the melody. It is dated January 1856.

I have often heard my father say that on a Sunday afternoon, in that month and year, he went for a walk up the Rhondda Road and that the melody then came to his mind. Returning to my grandfather's house, but a few doors from his own, he said to him, "Father, I have composed a melody which is in my opinion, a very fitting one for a Welsh patriotic song. Will you write some verses for it?"

"Let me hear it," said my grandfather. My father then sang the melody, and my grandfather said, "Fetch your harp, James." My father brought the harp to the Factory House and played the air on that instrument. My grandfather was greatly struck with it, and at once took down his slate which always hung by the side of his armchair by the fireplace and in a few minutes the words of the first verse were written. My father was singing the words to his melody, accompanying himself on the harp, when my grandmother returned home from evening service at Carmel Baptist Church, where she was a zealous and devoted member. She reprimanded my father severely for desecrating the Sabbath by playing the harp. He replied by saying to her, "Mam, cofiwch am y Brenin Dafydd yn chwarae ei delyn." ("Mam, remember King David playing his harp.") The second and third verse was written by the next day. The song became accordingly popular, so popular in fact that even the children were soon singing and whistling it in Pontypridd.

A prize was offered at the great Eisteddfod of Llangollen in 1858 for the best collection of unpublished Welsh airs. A friend of my father's, Mr Thomas Llewelyn (Llewelyn Alaw), a well known Welsh harpist and clever poet, decided to compete for this prize and with that in view called upon my father and asked him if he knew any unpublished Welsh airs. My father replied saying he did not, but one of his songs, which he called "Glanrhondda" in the original manuscript because I presume it was

141

composed on its banks, had become very popular, and if he (Mr Llewelyn) liked it, he could insert it in his collection with pleasure. My father was weaving at the time and he sang it to Mr Llewelyn from the loom, he (Mr Llewelyn) meanwhile sitting on a three-legged stool jotting down the notes. Mr Llewelyn added this song to his collection of unpublished Welsh Airs, competed at the Llangollen Eisteddfod and was awarded the first prize.

Owain Alaw, organist of Chester Cathedral, was the adjudicator and he, under the impression that it was an old song rescued from oblivion by Mr Llewelyn, published *Hen Wlad Fy Nhadau* in the third volume of his *"Gems of Welsh Melodies"*. My father and grandfather protested against this and Owain Alaw apologised to them and explained how the song came to be inserted in the *"Gems"*. Owain Alaw then asked for and obtained the permission of my father and grandfather to continue the insertion of *"Hen Wlad Fy Nhadau"* in the third vol. of *"The Gems Of Welsh Melodies"* which states that the song is published by <u>permission</u> of James James. Owain Alaw, some year after, offered to buy the copyright and offered my father <u>£15 worth of copies</u> of his (Owain Alaw) song *"Mae Robin yn Swil"*.

Don't you think this was a gross piece of impertinence after selling hundreds of copies of Vol. 3 of the *"Gems of Welsh Melodies"*? Mr Hughes of Wrexham, who published the *"Gems of Welsh Melodies"* for Owain Alaw called at the Factory, Pontypridd, on one occasion and told my father that more copies of Vol. 3 had been sold than Vols. 1 & 2 put together. Mr Hughes presented my father with the 3 Vols. and this is all he ever got for his song. <u>Nothing</u> from Owain Alaw who must have made hundreds of pounds out of father and grandfather's song.   The song that is now distinguished by the title of *"The Welsh National Anthem"*.

Yr eiddoch yn bur,
Taliesin James

Appendix 2

Owen Morgan, (Morien), gives the following account of how the anthem was composed in *History of Pontypridd and District* (1903). Morien claimed that this was how Evan James told the story to him when the poet was in his 70s:

"'It was,' said the Bard, 'on a Sunday evening, in January, 1856. My Wife and some of the children had gone to the service at Carmel Chapel and I was quite alone. I was brooding over thrilling incidents in the past history of Wales. My age at the time was 46 and James my eldest son, was 24 years old, and he played excellently on the harp. I had gone upstairs, intending to retire early, and was partly undressed when I heard James entering the house and then calling out, "Yn nhad, dewch i lawr yn union!" (Father, come down immediately!) The harper spoke so excitedly that I went down as I was.' 'I have been,' said James, 'for a stroll along the side of the Rhondda, and in the sound of its roar I have composed a new melody which has greatly moved me.' 'His face was aglow,' said the father. The father invited him to play it on his harp. The harp of Wales was brought forth to the middle of the room, then 'among the strings his fingers strayed' and with closed eyes the young Kimmerian sought to recall the notes which the dancing waters of the Rhondda had suggested to his soul. While thus engaged the mother returned from Mount Carmel conventicle and cried to James, 'what in the world is the meaning of this! Playing the harp on the Sunday night!' 'Mam annwyl,' replied James, 'don't forget King David played the harp of the tribe of Royal Judah in the house of the Lord.' Then the young harper of the Rhondda river bank caught the immortal strain and the mother and father looked on entranced."

Appendix 3

This version appears in *The Story of the National Anthem of Wales*, a published lecture given by Sir Alfred T. Davies, at the unveiling of a plaque in the Glyn Ceiriog Memorial Institute in 1942, thanking the father and son from Pontypridd for their gift to the people of Wales of a National Anthem:

"Evan James (Ieuan ap Iago, to give him the bardic title by which he was best known among his poetaster contemporaries) was a weaver by trade. Like many a Welshman, whether weaver, shoemaker, or shepherd, he mixed poetry with his work. One Saturday night, he 'sat musingly and thoughtfully' in his home at Pontypridd, in Glamorganshire. On the following (Sunday) morning he caused a message to be sent to his son James (Iago ap Ieuan) asking him to come to him and to bring with him his harp. Accordingly, in the evening, 'when the people were in Chapel,' his son, nothing loth, 'slipped down to his father's house' where later, on her return home his mother – finding him there with his beloved instrument, and doubtless playing it – sharply rebuked him. The rejoinder which she thereby brought upon herself, and which related to a certain Biblical incident, connected with David and his harp, seemingly closed further discussion on the subject, else the result might, perhaps, have been less happy for the world than, fortunately, proved to be the case.

"And so, it came about in this simple way and on that Sunday evening, whilst the father held in his hand the slate in which he was wont to jot down the thoughts which had surged through his mind during the day, the son swept the strings of his harp to the notes of the now imperishable melody which came to him as he did so. The older man, carefully adapting his words to the air, gave utterance to the theme which now forms part of the heritage of the Welsh people everywhere. Neither father nor son, in obedience to some over-powering influence, could free himself from the spell of a national sentiment which each wished to express. The song and the air are inseparably connected; they issued together as twins from the womb of thought. The first verse of 'Land of my Fathers' was finished that night; the second and third verses were added 'by early dawn of the next day.' Such is the simple story of the origin which its composers named 'Cwm (sic) Rhondda'."

Appendix 4

This is a report from the *Monmouthshire Merlin* of the Gelligaer Eisteddfod, held every year on Christmas Day. This was the eighth in that sequence of Eisteddfodau and took place either in 1848 or 1849.

Mr Evan James followed in a strain of attractive eloquence, in prose and verse; in the course of which he observed, that the present generation ought to exert themselves in every branch of literature to perpetuate their names, so that posterity may know that once such men had lived and had not thrown away their time. The Welsh, as a nation, had their antiquities, like other nations and he was glad to find that his brothers, the English, always gave commendation and credit to the Cambrian Triads – compositions of peculiar ability and wit. He was also glad to find that there was a Welsh monthly periodical about to be issued from the press at the beginning of the New Year, called the "Females of Wales", edited by the Rev Evan Jones[1]; and he would certainly, inasmuch as there had been such libellous allegations against the character and chastity of the fair sex belonging to Wales, exhort all present to become subscribers to it. (Loud cheers).

[1]Evan Jones (Ieuan Gwynedd 1820 – 52), was a native of Dolgellau and spent the last years of his life in Cardiff. He was buried at Groeswen, between Caerphilly and Pontypridd. He was active in the Temperance movement and fierce in his denunciation of the *Blue Books* commissioners. The monthly periodical was *Y Gymraes*. It is possible that this report was written by Ieuan Gwynedd himself, he was a regular contributor to the *Monmouthshire Merlin*.

144

Bibliography

Bebb, Ambrose: Pererindodau, Y Clwb Llyfrau Cymraeg (1941).

Bowen, Geraint: Golwg ar Orsedd y Beirdd, University of Wales Press (1992).

Edwards, Oswald: A Gem of Welsh Melody, Coelion Publications (1989).

Ellis, Tecwyn: Hen Wlad Fy Nhadau, **National Library of Wales Journal** (1954).

Evans, Meredydd: Who was "Orpheus" of the 1858 Llangollen Eisteddfod? In **Hanes Cerddoriaeth Cymru/History of Welsh Music** Volume 5 (2002), Editor Sally Harper.

Evans, Thomas: The History of Miskin Higher or The Parishes of Aberdare and Llanwynno, published by the author (1965).

Griffiths, Gwyn: Pontypridd in **Rhwng Dwy Afon**, Eisteddfod Genedlaethol Urdd Gobaith Cymru, Taf-Elái (1991), editor David A. Pretty.

Hughes, D. G. Lloyd: Anthem Genedlaethol y Cymry, Y Faner (August 3, 1984).

Huws, Daniel: Ieuan ab Iago. In **National Library of Wales Journal** (Winter, 1969).

Leyshon, Thomas Taliesin: Bridges to Harps to Millionaires (1993), Published by the author.

Miles, Dilwyn: The Secret of the Bards of the Isle of Britain, Dinefwr Press (1992).

Morse, Dafydd: Glanffrwd a 'Chlic y Bont' in **Rhwng Dwy Afon**, Eisteddfod Genedlaethol Urdd Gobaith Cymru, Taf-Elái (1991), editor David A. Pretty.

Morse, Dafydd: Thomas Williams (Brynfab, 1848-1927). In **Cwm Rhondda**, Gwasg Gomer (1995), editor Hywel Teifi Ewards.

Nicholas, W. Rhys: The Authors of 'Hen Wlad Fy Nhadau' from **The Bridge and the Song**, Mid-Glamorgan County Libraries (1991), editors P. F. Tobin and J. I. Davies.

Morgan, Owen (Morien): History of Pontypridd and District (1903).

Scholes, Percy A.: Hen Wlad Fy Nhadau. In **National Library of Wales Journal** (Summer, 1943).

Thomas, Mair Elvet: Afiaith yng Ngwent. University of Wales Press (1978).
.
Walters, Huw: Beirdd a Phrydyddion Pontypridd a'r Cylch yn y Bedwaredd Ganrif ar Bymtheg. In **Merthyr a Thaf**, Gwasg Gomer (2001), editor Hywel Teifi Edwards.

Walters, Huw: Cynnwrf Canrif. Barddas (2004).

Walters, Huw: Myfyr Morganwg and the Rocking-Stone Gorsedd. In **A Rattleskull Genius**, University of Wales Press (2005), editor Geraint H. Jenkins.

Webb, Harri: Our National Anthem. The Triskell Press (1964).

Williams, Griffith John: Traddodiad Llenyddol Morgannwg. University of Wales Press (1948).